50 Mexican Variety Recipes for Home

By: Kelly Johnson

Table of Contents

- Tacos al Pastor
- Chicken Enchiladas
- Beef Fajitas
- Shrimp Ceviche
- Chile Rellenos
- Carnitas
- Queso Fundido
- Guacamole
- Chicken Tortilla Soup
- Carne Asada
- Mexican Rice
- Refried Beans
- Salsa Verde
- Tamales
- Chilaquiles
- Pozole
- Fish Tacos
- Flan
- Horchata
- Tostadas
- Mole Poblano
- Barbacoa
- Sopes
- Pico de Gallo
- Chiles en Nogada
- Enchiladas Suizas
- Churros
- Cochinita Pibil
- Molletes
- Cactus Salad (Ensalada de Nopales)
- Mexican Street Corn (Elote)
- Empanadas
- Picadillo
- Tamale Pie
- Mexican Hot Chocolate

- Tinga de Pollo
- Mexican Wedding Cookies (Polvorones)
- Tlayudas
- Tres Leches Cake
- Camarones a la Diabla
- Pozole Verde
- Huevos Rancheros
- Pan de Muerto
- Frijoles Charros
- Mexican Fruit Salad (Ensalada de Frutas)
- Quesadillas
- Chicharrón en Salsa Verde
- Aguachile
- Capirotada (Mexican Bread Pudding)
- Chicken Tinga

Tacos al Pastor

Ingredients:

For the Marinade:

- 3-4 pounds pork shoulder, thinly sliced
- 3-4 dried guajillo chilies, stemmed and seeded
- 2-3 dried ancho chilies, stemmed and seeded
- 1 medium onion, roughly chopped
- 4 cloves garlic
- 1/4 cup pineapple juice
- 1/4 cup orange juice
- 1/4 cup white vinegar
- 1 tablespoon achiote paste (annatto paste)
- 1 tablespoon dried oregano
- 1 teaspoon ground cumin
- 1 teaspoon smoked paprika
- Salt and pepper, to taste

For Serving:

- Small corn tortillas
- Pineapple slices, grilled
- Chopped cilantro
- Diced onion
- Lime wedges
- Salsa verde or your favorite hot sauce

Instructions:

1. Prepare the Marinade: In a blender or food processor, combine the dried chilies, chopped onion, garlic, pineapple juice, orange juice, white vinegar, achiote paste, dried oregano, ground cumin, smoked paprika, salt, and pepper. Blend until smooth.
2. Marinate the Pork: Place the thinly sliced pork shoulder in a large bowl or resealable plastic bag. Pour the marinade over the pork, ensuring it's evenly

coated. Marinate in the refrigerator for at least 4 hours, or preferably overnight, to allow the flavors to develop.
3. Preheat the Grill: If using a grill, preheat it to medium-high heat. If using an oven, preheat it to 375°F (190°C).
4. Cook the Pork: Thread the marinated pork slices onto a vertical rotisserie skewer or place them on a baking sheet lined with parchment paper. If grilling, cook the pork on the rotisserie until cooked through and slightly charred, about 20–25 minutes, rotating occasionally for even cooking. If using an oven, roast the pork in the preheated oven until cooked through and slightly caramelized, about 25–30 minutes.
5. Assemble the Tacos: Warm the corn tortillas on a hot griddle or skillet until soft and pliable. Fill each tortilla with a few slices of the cooked pork, grilled pineapple slices, chopped cilantro, diced onion, and a squeeze of lime juice. Serve with salsa verde or your favorite hot sauce on the side.
6. Enjoy: Serve the Tacos al Pastor immediately while they're hot and enjoy the delicious flavors of this classic Mexican dish!

Feel free to adjust the level of spiciness and seasoning according to your taste preferences. These tacos are perfect for a casual dinner or a festive gathering with friends and family.

Chicken Enchiladas

Ingredients:

For the Enchilada Filling:

- 2 boneless, skinless chicken breasts
- 1 tablespoon olive oil
- 1 small onion, diced
- 2 cloves garlic, minced
- 1 teaspoon ground cumin
- 1 teaspoon chili powder
- 1/2 teaspoon paprika
- Salt and pepper, to taste
- 1 cup canned black beans, drained and rinsed
- 1 cup corn kernels (fresh, frozen, or canned)
- 1/4 cup chopped fresh cilantro
- 2 cups shredded Monterey Jack or Mexican blend cheese, divided
- 8-10 large flour tortillas or corn tortillas

For the Enchilada Sauce:

- 2 tablespoons olive oil
- 2 tablespoons all-purpose flour
- 4 tablespoons chili powder
- 1/2 teaspoon garlic powder
- 1/2 teaspoon onion powder
- 1/2 teaspoon ground cumin
- 1/4 teaspoon dried oregano
- 2 cups chicken or vegetable broth
- Salt and pepper, to taste

For Garnish:

- Chopped fresh cilantro
- Diced avocado
- Sliced jalapeños
- Sour cream

- Sliced green onions

Instructions:

1. Prepare the Chicken: Preheat the oven to 375°F (190°C). Season the chicken breasts with salt, pepper, ground cumin, chili powder, and paprika. In a skillet, heat olive oil over medium heat. Add the seasoned chicken breasts and cook until browned on both sides and cooked through, about 6-8 minutes per side. Remove from the skillet, let them cool slightly, and shred the chicken using two forks.
2. Make the Enchilada Filling: In the same skillet used for cooking the chicken, add a bit more olive oil if needed. Sauté the diced onion and minced garlic until softened, about 3-4 minutes. Add the shredded chicken back to the skillet along with black beans, corn, chopped cilantro, and 1 cup of shredded cheese. Stir until everything is well combined and the cheese is melted. Remove from heat.
3. Prepare the Enchilada Sauce: In a separate saucepan, heat olive oil over medium heat. Stir in the flour and chili powder to make a roux. Cook for 1 minute, stirring constantly. Gradually whisk in the chicken or vegetable broth until smooth. Stir in the garlic powder, onion powder, ground cumin, dried oregano, salt, and pepper. Simmer the sauce for 10-15 minutes, stirring occasionally, until it thickens slightly.
4. Assemble the Enchiladas: Spoon a small amount of enchilada sauce into the bottom of a baking dish to coat the bottom. Place a spoonful of the chicken filling onto each tortilla, roll it up tightly, and place it seam side down in the baking dish. Repeat with the remaining tortillas and filling.
5. Bake the Enchiladas: Pour the remaining enchilada sauce over the rolled tortillas in the baking dish, making sure to cover them evenly. Sprinkle the remaining shredded cheese on top. Cover the baking dish with aluminum foil and bake in the preheated oven for 20-25 minutes, or until the cheese is melted and bubbly.
6. Serve: Garnish the baked enchiladas with chopped fresh cilantro, diced avocado, sliced jalapeños, sour cream, and sliced green onions, if desired. Serve hot and enjoy!

These chicken enchiladas are a crowd-pleaser and perfect for a family dinner or potluck. Feel free to customize the filling with your favorite ingredients, such as bell peppers, spinach, or diced tomatoes.

Beef Fajitas

Ingredients:

For the Marinade:

- 1 ½ pounds flank steak or skirt steak, thinly sliced against the grain
- 1/4 cup olive oil
- 1/4 cup lime juice
- 3 cloves garlic, minced
- 2 tablespoons soy sauce
- 1 tablespoon Worcestershire sauce
- 1 tablespoon chili powder
- 1 teaspoon ground cumin
- 1 teaspoon smoked paprika
- 1/2 teaspoon dried oregano
- Salt and black pepper, to taste

For the Fajitas:

- 2 bell peppers (any color), thinly sliced
- 1 large onion, thinly sliced
- 2 tablespoons vegetable oil, for cooking
- 8-10 flour tortillas, warmed
- Optional toppings: sliced avocado, sour cream, shredded cheese, salsa, chopped cilantro, lime wedges

Instructions:

1. Marinate the Beef: In a large bowl or resealable plastic bag, combine the olive oil, lime juice, minced garlic, soy sauce, Worcestershire sauce, chili powder, ground cumin, smoked paprika, dried oregano, salt, and black pepper. Add the thinly sliced beef to the marinade and toss until well coated. Cover the bowl or seal the bag, and refrigerate for at least 1 hour, or preferably overnight, to allow the flavors to meld.
2. Prepare the Vegetables: In a separate bowl, toss the thinly sliced bell peppers and onions with a tablespoon of vegetable oil. Season with salt and pepper to taste.

3. Cook the Beef and Vegetables: Heat a large skillet or grill pan over medium-high heat. Once hot, add the marinated beef in batches and cook for 2-3 minutes per side, or until browned and cooked to your desired doneness. Transfer the cooked beef to a plate and cover with aluminum foil to keep warm.
4. In the same skillet or grill pan, add the seasoned bell peppers and onions. Cook, stirring occasionally, until the vegetables are tender and slightly charred, about 5-7 minutes.
5. Assemble the Fajitas: Warm the flour tortillas in a dry skillet or wrap them in aluminum foil and heat them in the oven for a few minutes. Fill each tortilla with a portion of the cooked beef and grilled vegetables.
6. Add Toppings: Garnish the beef fajitas with your favorite toppings, such as sliced avocado, sour cream, shredded cheese, salsa, chopped cilantro, and a squeeze of lime juice.
7. Serve: Serve the beef fajitas immediately while warm, and enjoy!

Beef fajitas are versatile and can be customized according to your preferences. Feel free to add additional toppings or adjust the seasoning to suit your taste.

Shrimp Ceviche

Ingredients:

- 1 pound fresh shrimp, peeled, deveined, and chopped into bite-sized pieces
- 1 cup fresh lime juice (about 6-8 limes)
- 1 cup fresh lemon juice (about 4 lemons)
- 1 small red onion, finely diced
- 1 cucumber, seeded and finely diced
- 1 jalapeño pepper, seeded and finely diced
- 1 tomato, seeded and finely diced
- 1/4 cup chopped fresh cilantro
- 2 tablespoons chopped fresh parsley
- Salt and pepper, to taste
- Tortilla chips or crackers, for serving
- Avocado slices, for garnish (optional)

Instructions:

1. Prepare the Shrimp: In a large bowl, combine the chopped shrimp with the fresh lime juice and fresh lemon juice. Make sure the shrimp is fully submerged in the citrus juices. Cover the bowl and refrigerate for at least 30 minutes, or until the shrimp turns opaque and pink. This process "cooks" the shrimp through the acidity of the citrus juices.
2. Prepare the Vegetables: While the shrimp is marinating, prepare the vegetables. Finely dice the red onion, cucumber, jalapeño pepper, and tomato. Chop the fresh cilantro and parsley. Place all the diced vegetables and herbs in a separate bowl.
3. Combine the Ingredients: Once the shrimp is "cooked" in the citrus juices, drain off most of the excess liquid, leaving just enough to keep the ceviche moist. Add the diced vegetables and herbs to the bowl with the shrimp. Gently toss to combine.
4. Season the Ceviche: Season the shrimp ceviche with salt and pepper to taste. Adjust the seasoning as needed.
5. Chill: Cover the bowl of shrimp ceviche and refrigerate for at least 15-20 minutes to allow the flavors to meld together.
6. Serve: When ready to serve, transfer the shrimp ceviche to a serving bowl. Garnish with avocado slices, if desired. Serve chilled with tortilla chips or crackers on the side.

7. Enjoy: Serve the shrimp ceviche immediately and enjoy its fresh and vibrant flavors!

Shrimp ceviche is best enjoyed fresh, so try to consume it soon after preparing. It's a delightful appetizer for gatherings or a light and healthy snack any time of the day.

Chile Rellenos

Ingredients:

For the Chile Rellenos:

- 4 large poblano peppers
- 8 ounces Monterey Jack cheese or Oaxaca cheese, cut into strips
- All-purpose flour, for dredging
- Vegetable oil, for frying

For the Egg Batter:

- 4 large eggs, separated
- 1/2 teaspoon salt
- 1/4 teaspoon black pepper

For the Tomato Sauce:

- 2 tablespoons vegetable oil
- 1 small onion, finely chopped
- 2 cloves garlic, minced
- 2 cups canned diced tomatoes
- 1 teaspoon dried oregano
- 1/2 teaspoon ground cumin
- Salt and pepper, to taste

For Garnish:

- Chopped fresh cilantro
- Sour cream or Mexican crema
- Sliced avocado
- Lime wedges

Instructions:

1. Roast and Peel the Poblano Peppers: Preheat the broiler in your oven. Place the poblano peppers on a baking sheet and broil, turning occasionally, until the skins are charred and blistered all over, about 5-7 minutes. Transfer the roasted peppers to a bowl and cover with plastic wrap or a clean kitchen towel. Let them steam for about 10 minutes. Once cooled, peel off the charred skin, make a small slit along one side of each pepper, and remove the seeds and membranes.
2. Stuff the Peppers: Carefully stuff each poblano pepper with strips of cheese. Be sure not to overfill them.
3. Prepare the Egg Batter: In a large bowl, beat the egg whites until stiff peaks form. In a separate bowl, beat the egg yolks with salt and pepper until smooth. Gently fold the beaten egg yolks into the egg whites until just combined.
4. Coat the Peppers: Lightly dredge each stuffed poblano pepper in flour, shaking off any excess. Then, dip the peppers into the egg batter, making sure they're evenly coated.
5. Fry the Chile Rellenos: In a large skillet, heat vegetable oil over medium heat until hot but not smoking. Carefully place the battered peppers in the hot oil and fry until golden brown on all sides, about 3-4 minutes per side. Transfer the fried chile rellenos to a plate lined with paper towels to drain excess oil.
6. Make the Tomato Sauce: In a separate saucepan, heat vegetable oil over medium heat. Add chopped onion and garlic, and cook until softened, about 3-4 minutes. Stir in diced tomatoes, dried oregano, ground cumin, salt, and pepper. Simmer the sauce for 10-15 minutes, stirring occasionally, until slightly thickened.
7. Serve: Serve the Chile Rellenos hot with the tomato sauce spooned over the top. Garnish with chopped fresh cilantro, sour cream or Mexican crema, sliced avocado, and lime wedges on the side.
8. Enjoy: Serve immediately and enjoy the delicious flavors of homemade Chile Rellenos!

Chile Rellenos are a delightful dish that combines the smoky flavor of roasted poblanos with creamy melted cheese and a crispy egg batter. It's a perfect choice for a festive dinner or special occasion.

Carnitas

Ingredients:

- 3-4 pounds pork shoulder (also known as pork butt), cut into large chunks
- 1 onion, quartered
- 4 cloves garlic, smashed
- 2 bay leaves
- 1 teaspoon dried oregano
- 1 teaspoon ground cumin
- 1 teaspoon smoked paprika
- 1 teaspoon chili powder
- 1 teaspoon salt
- 1/2 teaspoon black pepper
- 1 orange, juiced
- 1 lime, juiced
- 1/4 cup vegetable oil or lard
- 1/2 cup water

Instructions:

1. Prepare the Pork: Trim excess fat from the pork shoulder and cut it into large chunks, about 2-inch pieces.
2. Season the Pork: In a large bowl, combine the pork chunks with quartered onion, smashed garlic cloves, bay leaves, dried oregano, ground cumin, smoked paprika, chili powder, salt, and black pepper. Squeeze the juice of one orange and one lime over the pork. Mix well to coat the pork evenly with the seasoning. Let it marinate for at least 30 minutes, or refrigerate overnight for best results.
3. Cook the Carnitas: Heat vegetable oil or lard in a large Dutch oven or heavy-bottomed pot over medium-high heat. Once hot, add the marinated pork chunks in a single layer, working in batches if necessary to avoid overcrowding the pot. Brown the pork on all sides, about 3-4 minutes per side.
4. Braise the Pork: Once all the pork is browned, return it all to the pot. Add 1/2 cup of water to the pot. Bring it to a simmer, then reduce the heat to low. Cover and simmer gently for 2-3 hours, or until the pork is tender and easily shreds with a fork. Check occasionally and add more water if needed to prevent it from drying out.
5. Shred the Pork: Once the pork is tender, use two forks to shred it into bite-sized pieces. Increase the heat to medium-high and continue cooking, uncovered,

stirring occasionally, until the pork is golden brown and crispy in spots, about 10-15 minutes.
6. **Serve:** Serve the carnitas hot as a filling for tacos, burritos, or as a topping for rice bowls. Garnish with chopped cilantro, diced onions, salsa, avocado, and lime wedges if desired.
7. **Enjoy:** Enjoy the delicious, tender, and flavorful carnitas with your favorite accompaniments!

Carnitas are perfect for a casual dinner or for feeding a crowd at gatherings. They're also great for meal prepping as they can be made ahead of time and reheated when ready to serve.

Queso Fundido

Ingredients:

- 8 ounces Mexican melting cheese (such as Oaxaca, Chihuahua, or Asadero), shredded
- 4 ounces Monterey Jack cheese, shredded
- 2 tablespoons vegetable oil or butter
- 1 small onion, finely chopped
- 2 cloves garlic, minced
- 1 jalapeño pepper, seeded and finely chopped (optional)
- 1 tomato, seeded and diced
- 1/4 cup chopped fresh cilantro
- 1/4 teaspoon ground cumin
- Salt and pepper, to taste
- Tortilla chips or warm tortillas, for serving

Instructions:

1. Prepare the Cheese: In a bowl, mix together the shredded Mexican melting cheese and Monterey Jack cheese. Set aside.
2. Sauté the Aromatics: Heat vegetable oil or butter in a skillet over medium heat. Add finely chopped onion and cook until softened, about 3-4 minutes. Add minced garlic and chopped jalapeño pepper (if using), and cook for another 1-2 minutes until fragrant.
3. Add Tomatoes and Cilantro: Stir in diced tomatoes and chopped cilantro. Cook for another 2-3 minutes until the tomatoes soften slightly.
4. Melt the Cheese: Reduce the heat to low. Gradually add the shredded cheese mixture to the skillet, stirring constantly, until the cheese is melted and smooth. Be careful not to let the cheese burn.
5. Season: Season the Queso Fundido with ground cumin, salt, and pepper to taste. Adjust the seasoning as needed.
6. Serve: Transfer the melted cheese mixture to a serving dish or a heatproof skillet. Serve immediately while hot, with tortilla chips or warm tortillas for dipping.
7. Enjoy: Dig into the warm, gooey Queso Fundido with your favorite dippers and enjoy the cheesy goodness!

Queso Fundido is perfect for parties, game nights, or as a comforting snack. Feel free to customize it with your favorite ingredients such as cooked chorizo, diced green chilies, or roasted poblano peppers.

Guacamole

Ingredients:

- 3 ripe avocados
- 1 lime, juiced
- 1/4 cup finely chopped red onion
- 1-2 cloves garlic, minced
- 1-2 tablespoons chopped fresh cilantro
- 1 jalapeño pepper, seeded and finely chopped (optional, for heat)
- 1 medium tomato, diced (optional)
- Salt and pepper, to taste

Instructions:

1. Prepare the Avocados: Cut the avocados in half and remove the pits. Scoop the avocado flesh into a medium-sized bowl.
2. Mash the Avocado: Use a fork or potato masher to mash the avocado until it reaches your desired consistency. Some people prefer it chunky, while others prefer it smoother.
3. Add Lime Juice: Squeeze the juice of one lime over the mashed avocado. This not only adds flavor but also helps prevent the avocado from browning too quickly.
4. Add Onion, Garlic, and Cilantro: Add the finely chopped red onion, minced garlic, and chopped fresh cilantro to the bowl. Stir to combine.
5. Add Jalapeño and Tomato (Optional): If you like a bit of heat and extra texture, add finely chopped jalapeño pepper and diced tomato to the guacamole. Stir to combine.
6. Season: Season the guacamole with salt and pepper to taste. Adjust the seasoning as needed.
7. Chill (Optional): If you have time, cover the guacamole with plastic wrap, pressing it directly onto the surface to prevent browning, and refrigerate for 30 minutes to allow the flavors to meld together.
8. Serve: Transfer the guacamole to a serving bowl. Garnish with additional chopped cilantro or a slice of lime if desired. Serve with tortilla chips, tacos, burritos, or your favorite Mexican dishes.
9. Enjoy: Dive into the creamy, flavorful goodness of homemade guacamole and enjoy it as a snack, appetizer, or accompaniment to your favorite dishes!

Guacamole is best enjoyed fresh but can be stored in an airtight container in the refrigerator for up to a day. If storing leftovers, place a piece of plastic wrap directly on the surface of the guacamole to prevent oxidation and browning.

Chicken Tortilla Soup

Ingredients:

For the Soup:

- 1 tablespoon olive oil
- 1 onion, diced
- 2 cloves garlic, minced
- 1 jalapeño pepper, seeded and diced
- 1 red bell pepper, diced
- 1 carrot, diced
- 1 teaspoon ground cumin
- 1 teaspoon chili powder
- 1/2 teaspoon paprika
- 1/2 teaspoon dried oregano
- Salt and pepper, to taste
- 4 cups chicken broth
- 1 (14.5-ounce) can diced tomatoes
- 1 cup cooked shredded chicken (rotisserie chicken works well)
- 1 (15-ounce) can black beans, drained and rinsed
- 1 cup frozen corn kernels
- Juice of 1 lime
- Chopped fresh cilantro, for garnish

For the Tortilla Strips:

- 4 corn tortillas, cut into thin strips
- 1 tablespoon olive oil
- Salt, to taste

For Garnish:

- Sliced avocado
- Sour cream or Mexican crema
- Shredded cheese (such as Monterey Jack or cheddar)

- Lime wedges
- Additional chopped cilantro
- Sliced jalapeños (optional)

Instructions:

1. Prepare the Tortilla Strips: Preheat the oven to 375°F (190°C). Toss the corn tortilla strips with olive oil and a pinch of salt. Spread them in a single layer on a baking sheet. Bake in the preheated oven for 10-12 minutes, or until crispy and golden brown. Set aside.
2. Make the Soup: In a large pot or Dutch oven, heat olive oil over medium heat. Add diced onion, minced garlic, diced jalapeño pepper, diced red bell pepper, and diced carrot. Cook, stirring occasionally, until the vegetables are softened, about 5-7 minutes.
3. Add ground cumin, chili powder, paprika, dried oregano, salt, and pepper to the pot. Stir to coat the vegetables in the spices.
4. Pour in the chicken broth and diced tomatoes with their juices. Bring the soup to a simmer.
5. Add cooked shredded chicken, black beans, and frozen corn kernels to the pot. Simmer for another 10-15 minutes, or until the flavors are well combined and the soup is heated through.
6. Stir in the lime juice and chopped fresh cilantro. Taste and adjust the seasoning, if needed.
7. Serve: Ladle the chicken tortilla soup into bowls. Top each serving with crispy tortilla strips and garnish with sliced avocado, sour cream or Mexican crema, shredded cheese, lime wedges, additional chopped cilantro, and sliced jalapeños, if desired.
8. Enjoy: Serve hot and enjoy the comforting flavors of homemade chicken tortilla soup!

This soup is perfect for chilly days or anytime you're craving a comforting and satisfying meal. Feel free to customize it by adding other ingredients like diced tomatoes, green chilies, or cooked rice.

Carne Asada

Ingredients:

For the Marinade:

- 2 pounds flank steak or skirt steak
- 1/4 cup orange juice
- 1/4 cup lime juice
- 1/4 cup soy sauce
- 4 cloves garlic, minced
- 1/4 cup chopped fresh cilantro
- 2 tablespoons vegetable oil
- 1 teaspoon ground cumin
- 1 teaspoon chili powder
- 1 teaspoon smoked paprika
- 1 teaspoon dried oregano
- Salt and pepper, to taste

For Serving:

- Warm tortillas (corn or flour)
- Chopped fresh cilantro
- Diced onions
- Sliced avocado or guacamole
- Lime wedges

Instructions:

1. Prepare the Marinade: In a bowl, whisk together orange juice, lime juice, soy sauce, minced garlic, chopped cilantro, vegetable oil, ground cumin, chili powder, smoked paprika, dried oregano, salt, and pepper.
2. Marinate the Steak: Place the flank steak or skirt steak in a shallow dish or resealable plastic bag. Pour the marinade over the steak, making sure it's evenly coated. Cover the dish or seal the bag, and refrigerate for at least 4 hours, or overnight for best results. Turn the steak occasionally to ensure all sides are evenly marinated.

3. Preheat the Grill: Preheat your grill to medium-high heat. If using a stovetop grill pan or skillet, heat it over medium-high heat until hot.
4. Grill the Steak: Remove the marinated steak from the refrigerator and let it sit at room temperature for about 20-30 minutes. Drain excess marinade from the steak. Grill the steak over direct heat for 4-6 minutes per side, or until it reaches your desired level of doneness. For medium-rare, the internal temperature should register 130-135°F (55-57°C) on a meat thermometer.
5. Rest the Steak: Transfer the grilled steak to a cutting board and let it rest for 5-10 minutes. This allows the juices to redistribute and ensures a tender and juicy steak.
6. Slice the Steak: After resting, slice the steak against the grain into thin strips. This helps break down the muscle fibers and ensures tender slices.
7. Serve: Serve the carne asada slices with warm tortillas. Garnish with chopped fresh cilantro, diced onions, sliced avocado or guacamole, and lime wedges on the side.
8. Enjoy: Build your own tacos or burritos by filling the warm tortillas with the sliced carne asada and your favorite toppings. Squeeze some fresh lime juice over the top for an extra burst of flavor.

Carne Asada is a delicious and versatile dish that's perfect for a casual weeknight dinner or for entertaining guests at a barbecue. Adjust the seasoning and level of heat to suit your taste preferences.

Mexican Rice

Ingredients:

- 1 cup long-grain white rice
- 1 tablespoon vegetable oil or olive oil
- 1 small onion, finely chopped
- 2 cloves garlic, minced
- 1 cup canned diced tomatoes (with juices)
- 1 3/4 cups chicken or vegetable broth
- 1 teaspoon ground cumin
- 1/2 teaspoon chili powder
- 1/2 teaspoon paprika
- Salt and pepper, to taste
- Chopped fresh cilantro, for garnish (optional)

Instructions:

1. Rinse the Rice: Place the rice in a fine-mesh sieve and rinse it under cold water until the water runs clear. This helps remove excess starch and prevents the rice from becoming too sticky when cooked.
2. Sauté the Aromatics: In a large skillet or saucepan, heat the vegetable oil over medium heat. Add the chopped onion and minced garlic, and sauté until softened and fragrant, about 3-4 minutes.
3. Toast the Rice: Add the rinsed rice to the skillet with the onions and garlic. Cook, stirring constantly, until the rice is lightly toasted and golden brown, about 3-4 minutes.
4. Add the Tomatoes and Broth: Stir in the diced tomatoes with their juices. Cook for another 1-2 minutes, allowing the flavors to meld. Then, pour in the chicken or vegetable broth, and add ground cumin, chili powder, paprika, salt, and pepper to taste. Stir well to combine.
5. Simmer the Rice: Bring the mixture to a boil, then reduce the heat to low. Cover the skillet with a tight-fitting lid and simmer for 15-20 minutes, or until the rice is tender and has absorbed all the liquid. Avoid lifting the lid during this time to ensure proper cooking.
6. Fluff the Rice: Once the rice is cooked, remove the skillet from the heat and let it sit, covered, for an additional 5 minutes to allow the steam to redistribute. Then, uncover the skillet and fluff the rice with a fork.

7. Garnish and Serve: Transfer the Mexican rice to a serving dish. Garnish with chopped fresh cilantro, if desired, for a pop of color and flavor. Serve hot as a side dish alongside your favorite Mexican entrees.
8. Enjoy: Enjoy the aromatic and flavorful Mexican rice as a delicious accompaniment to tacos, enchiladas, burritos, or any other Mexican-inspired dishes!

This homemade Mexican rice is easy to prepare and much tastier than store-bought versions. Feel free to customize it with additional vegetables, such as bell peppers or corn, for added texture and flavor.

Refried Beans

Ingredients:

- 2 cups cooked pinto beans (or black beans), drained and rinsed
- 2 tablespoons lard, bacon fat, or vegetable oil
- 1/2 onion, finely chopped
- 2 cloves garlic, minced
- 1 teaspoon ground cumin
- 1/2 teaspoon chili powder (optional)
- Salt and pepper, to taste
- 1/4 cup water (or bean cooking liquid)

Instructions:

1. Heat Fat: In a large skillet or frying pan, heat the lard, bacon fat, or vegetable oil over medium heat until melted and hot.
2. Sauté Onion and Garlic: Add the finely chopped onion to the skillet and sauté until softened and translucent, about 3-4 minutes. Add the minced garlic and cook for an additional minute until fragrant.
3. Add Beans: Add the cooked pinto beans (or black beans) to the skillet. Using a potato masher or the back of a spoon, mash the beans until they are mostly smooth but still slightly chunky.
4. Season: Stir in the ground cumin, chili powder (if using), salt, and pepper to taste. Adjust the seasoning according to your preference.
5. Add Water: Pour in the water (or bean cooking liquid) to the skillet to loosen the beans and prevent them from drying out. Stir well to combine.
6. Simmer: Reduce the heat to low and simmer the refried beans for 5-7 minutes, stirring occasionally, until heated through and the flavors are well blended. If the beans become too thick, add more water as needed to achieve your desired consistency.
7. Adjust Consistency: If you prefer smoother refried beans, you can continue mashing and stirring them until they reach the desired texture. For thicker beans, cook them for a few minutes longer to allow excess liquid to evaporate.
8. Serve: Once the refried beans are heated through and have reached your desired consistency, remove the skillet from the heat. Transfer the beans to a serving bowl and serve hot.

9. Enjoy: Enjoy the delicious and flavorful refried beans as a side dish or use them as a filling for your favorite Mexican dishes such as burritos, tacos, tostadas, or enchiladas!

This homemade refried beans recipe is simple to make and much tastier than store-bought versions. Feel free to customize it by adding diced jalapeños, chopped cilantro, or crumbled queso fresco for extra flavor and texture.

Salsa Verde

Ingredients:

- 1 pound tomatillos, husks removed and rinsed
- 2-3 serrano or jalapeño peppers, stemmed (adjust based on desired spice level)
- 1 small onion, chopped
- 2 cloves garlic
- 1/4 cup chopped fresh cilantro
- Juice of 1 lime
- Salt, to taste

Instructions:

1. Roast the Tomatillos and Peppers: Preheat the broiler in your oven. Place the tomatillos and peppers on a baking sheet and broil, turning occasionally, until charred and softened, about 8-10 minutes. Alternatively, you can roast them on a hot grill or stovetop grill pan until charred and softened.
2. Blend Ingredients: Transfer the roasted tomatillos and peppers to a blender or food processor. Add chopped onion, garlic, cilantro, and lime juice to the blender. Blend until smooth.
3. Adjust Seasoning: Taste the salsa verde and season with salt to taste. Adjust the amount of lime juice or add more cilantro if desired.
4. Serve: Transfer the salsa verde to a serving bowl or jar. Serve immediately or refrigerate until ready to use. The flavors will meld together even more if allowed to sit for a few hours or overnight.
5. Enjoy: Use salsa verde as a dip with tortilla chips, or as a sauce for tacos, enchiladas, grilled meats, or seafood. It adds a tangy and spicy kick to any dish!

This homemade salsa verde recipe is easy to make and can be customized based on your preferences. You can adjust the spiciness by adding more or fewer chili peppers, and you can also experiment with adding other ingredients such as roasted garlic or roasted poblano peppers for additional flavor complexity.

Tamales

Ingredients:

For the Filling:

- 1 pound pork shoulder or pork butt, trimmed and cut into chunks
- 1 onion, chopped
- 2 cloves garlic, minced
- 1 teaspoon ground cumin
- 1 teaspoon dried oregano
- 1 teaspoon chili powder
- Salt and pepper, to taste
- 2 cups chicken broth or water

For the Masa Dough:

- 2 cups masa harina (corn flour)
- 1 teaspoon baking powder
- 1/2 teaspoon salt
- 1 1/4 cups chicken broth or water
- 2/3 cup lard or vegetable shortening

For Assembling:

- Dried corn husks, soaked in warm water for 1-2 hours and drained
- Prepared pork filling
- Prepared masa dough

Instructions:

Prepare the Filling:

1. In a large pot or Dutch oven, combine the pork chunks, chopped onion, minced garlic, ground cumin, dried oregano, chili powder, salt, pepper, and chicken broth or water.
2. Bring the mixture to a boil over medium-high heat. Reduce the heat to low, cover, and simmer for 2-3 hours, or until the pork is tender and easily shreds with a fork.
3. Remove the pork from the pot and shred it using two forks. Return the shredded pork to the pot and simmer for another 30 minutes to allow the flavors to meld together. Adjust seasoning if needed. Set aside.

Prepare the Masa Dough:

1. In a large mixing bowl, combine the masa harina, baking powder, and salt.
2. Gradually add the chicken broth or water to the dry ingredients, mixing until a soft dough forms.
3. In a separate bowl, beat the lard or vegetable shortening until light and fluffy. Gradually add the beaten lard to the masa dough, mixing until well combined and smooth.

Assemble the Tamales:

1. Pat dry the soaked corn husks with a clean kitchen towel. Place a corn husk flat on your work surface with the narrow end facing you.
2. Spread about 2 tablespoons of the masa dough onto the center of the corn husk, leaving a border around the edges.
3. Spoon a tablespoon of the prepared pork filling down the center of the masa dough.
4. Fold the sides of the corn husk over the filling, then fold up the bottom to enclose the filling completely. Secure the tamale by tying it with a thin strip of corn husk or kitchen twine, if desired. Repeat with the remaining corn husks, masa dough, and filling.

Steam the Tamales:

1. Arrange the assembled tamales upright in a steamer basket, open-side up.
2. Fill the bottom of the steamer pot with water, making sure it doesn't touch the tamales. Cover the pot with a lid.

3. Steam the tamales over medium heat for 1 to 1 1/2 hours, or until the masa dough is firm and pulls away easily from the corn husks.
4. Check the water level periodically and add more water as needed to prevent it from drying out.

Serve:

1. Allow the tamales to cool slightly before serving.
2. To serve, unwrap the tamales from the corn husks and enjoy them warm with your favorite toppings such as salsa, guacamole, or sour cream.
3. Leftover tamales can be stored in the refrigerator for a few days or frozen for longer storage. Reheat them by steaming or microwaving until heated through.

Enjoy these delicious homemade pork tamales as a festive and satisfying meal!

Chilaquiles

Ingredients:

For the Sauce:

- 2 tablespoons vegetable oil
- 1 onion, chopped
- 2 cloves garlic, minced
- 2 jalapeño peppers, seeded and chopped
- 2 cups diced tomatoes (fresh or canned)
- 1 (4-ounce) can diced green chilies
- 1 teaspoon ground cumin
- 1 teaspoon chili powder
- 1/2 teaspoon paprika
- Salt and pepper, to taste
- 1 cup chicken broth or water

For the Chilaquiles:

- 6 cups tortilla chips or homemade fried tortilla strips
- 1 cup shredded cooked chicken or cooked chorizo (optional)
- 1 cup shredded cheese (such as Monterey Jack or cheddar)
- 1/4 cup chopped fresh cilantro
- 2-3 eggs (optional)
- Sliced avocado, sour cream, lime wedges, for serving

Instructions:

Prepare the Sauce:

1. In a large skillet or saucepan, heat the vegetable oil over medium heat. Add the chopped onion and cook until softened, about 3-4 minutes.
2. Add the minced garlic and chopped jalapeño peppers to the skillet. Cook for another 1-2 minutes until fragrant.

3. Stir in the diced tomatoes, diced green chilies, ground cumin, chili powder, paprika, salt, and pepper. Cook for 5-7 minutes, stirring occasionally, until the tomatoes start to break down and release their juices.
4. Pour in the chicken broth or water and bring the sauce to a simmer. Reduce the heat to low and let it simmer for 10-15 minutes, stirring occasionally, until the sauce thickens slightly. Adjust seasoning if needed.

Assemble the Chilaquiles:

1. Add the tortilla chips or homemade fried tortilla strips to the skillet with the sauce. Gently toss until the chips are evenly coated with the sauce.
2. If using, add the shredded cooked chicken or cooked chorizo to the skillet and toss to combine.
3. Sprinkle the shredded cheese over the top of the chilaquiles. Cover the skillet with a lid and let it cook for 3-4 minutes, or until the cheese is melted and bubbly.
4. If desired, make wells in the chilaquiles and crack the eggs directly into the skillet. Cover and cook for an additional 3-5 minutes, or until the eggs are cooked to your liking.
5. Sprinkle chopped fresh cilantro over the top of the chilaquiles.

Serve:

1. Remove the skillet from the heat and serve the chilaquiles immediately.
2. Garnish with sliced avocado, dollops of sour cream, and lime wedges on the side.
3. Enjoy the delicious and comforting chilaquiles as a hearty breakfast, brunch, or anytime meal!

Chilaquiles are versatile, so feel free to customize them with your favorite toppings and add-ins. They're a great way to use up leftover tortilla chips or stale tortillas, and you can adjust the level of spiciness to suit your taste preferences.

Pozole

Ingredients:

For the Pozole:

- 2 pounds pork shoulder or pork butt, cut into chunks
- 1 onion, chopped
- 4 cloves garlic, minced
- 2 bay leaves
- 1 teaspoon dried oregano
- 1 teaspoon ground cumin
- 1 teaspoon chili powder
- Salt, to taste
- 8 cups water or chicken broth
- 2 (15-ounce) cans hominy, drained and rinsed

For Serving:

- Thinly sliced cabbage or lettuce
- Chopped fresh cilantro
- Diced onion
- Sliced radishes
- Lime wedges
- Avocado slices
- Tortilla chips or tostadas

Instructions:

1. Prepare the Pork: In a large pot or Dutch oven, combine the pork chunks, chopped onion, minced garlic, bay leaves, dried oregano, ground cumin, chili powder, and salt to taste.
2. Cook the Pork: Add water or chicken broth to the pot, enough to cover the pork by at least an inch. Bring the mixture to a boil over medium-high heat, then reduce the heat to low. Cover and simmer for 1 1/2 to 2 hours, or until the pork is tender and falls apart easily.

3. Shred the Pork: Remove the pork from the pot and shred it using two forks. Return the shredded pork to the pot.
4. Add Hominy: Add the drained and rinsed hominy to the pot with the shredded pork. Stir to combine.
5. Simmer: Simmer the pozole uncovered for an additional 30 minutes to allow the flavors to meld together and the hominy to soften.
6. Adjust Seasoning: Taste the pozole and adjust the seasoning with more salt if needed.
7. Serve: Ladle the pozole into serving bowls. Serve hot with thinly sliced cabbage or lettuce, chopped fresh cilantro, diced onion, sliced radishes, lime wedges, avocado slices, and tortilla chips or tostadas on the side.
8. Enjoy: Enjoy the comforting and flavorful pork pozole with all the delicious toppings!

Pozole is a versatile dish, so feel free to customize it with your favorite toppings and add-ins. You can also use different types of meat such as chicken or beef, or make a vegetarian version by omitting the meat and using vegetable broth instead.

Fish Tacos

Ingredients:

For the Fish:

- 1 pound white fish fillets (such as tilapia, cod, or mahi-mahi)
- 2 tablespoons olive oil
- 1 teaspoon chili powder
- 1/2 teaspoon ground cumin
- 1/2 teaspoon smoked paprika
- Salt and pepper, to taste
- Lime wedges, for serving

For Serving:

- 8 small corn or flour tortillas
- Shredded cabbage or lettuce
- Sliced avocado or guacamole
- Chopped fresh cilantro
- Diced tomatoes or pico de gallo
- Sliced radishes
- Sour cream or Mexican crema
- Hot sauce (such as chipotle or salsa verde)

Instructions:

1. Prepare the Fish:
    - If using large fish fillets, cut them into smaller pieces suitable for tacos.
    - In a small bowl, mix together olive oil, chili powder, cumin, smoked paprika, salt, and pepper to create a marinade.
    - Rub the marinade over the fish fillets, ensuring they are evenly coated. Let the fish marinate for at least 15-30 minutes to allow the flavors to penetrate.
2. Cook the Fish:
    - Heat a grill pan or skillet over medium-high heat. Brush the pan with a bit of oil to prevent sticking.

- Once the pan is hot, add the fish fillets and cook for 3-4 minutes on each side, or until the fish is cooked through and flakes easily with a fork. Cooking time may vary depending on the thickness of the fish.
3. Warm the Tortillas:
    - While the fish is cooking, warm the tortillas on a separate skillet or in the microwave according to the package instructions. Keep them warm and covered with a clean kitchen towel.
4. Assemble the Tacos:
    - Place a portion of cooked fish onto each warmed tortilla.
    - Top the fish with shredded cabbage or lettuce, sliced avocado or guacamole, chopped cilantro, diced tomatoes or pico de gallo, and sliced radishes.
    - Drizzle with sour cream or Mexican crema and add a dash of hot sauce, if desired.
    - Squeeze fresh lime juice over the top of each taco for a burst of citrus flavor.
5. Serve:
    - Serve the fish tacos immediately, accompanied by lime wedges on the side.
6. Enjoy:
    - Enjoy the delicious and flavorful fish tacos with your favorite toppings and sauces!

Feel free to customize your fish tacos with additional toppings such as diced onions, crumbled queso fresco, or salsa verde. Serve them alongside rice and beans for a complete meal, or enjoy them as a light and satisfying snack or appetizer.

Flan

Ingredients:

For the Caramel:

- 1 cup granulated sugar
- 1/4 cup water

For the Flan:

- 4 large eggs
- 1 can (14 ounces) sweetened condensed milk
- 1 can (12 ounces) evaporated milk
- 1 teaspoon vanilla extract
- Pinch of salt

Instructions:

1. Prepare the Caramel:
    - In a small saucepan, combine the granulated sugar and water over medium heat. Stir until the sugar is dissolved.
    - Once the sugar has dissolved, stop stirring and allow the mixture to come to a boil. Let it boil without stirring until it turns a deep amber color, about 5-7 minutes. Swirl the pan occasionally to ensure even caramelization.
    - Once the caramel reaches the desired color, immediately remove it from the heat and pour it into a round cake pan or individual ramekins, tilting the pan to coat the bottom evenly. Be careful as the caramel will be very hot. Quickly swirl the caramel around the sides of the pan or ramekins if desired. Set aside to cool and harden.
2. Preheat the Oven:
    - Preheat your oven to 350°F (175°C). Place a large baking dish or roasting pan in the oven and fill it with about 1 inch of hot water. This will create a water bath for baking the flan.
3. Make the Flan Mixture:
    - In a large mixing bowl, whisk together the eggs, sweetened condensed milk, evaporated milk, vanilla extract, and a pinch of salt until well

combined and smooth. Be careful not to overmix to avoid incorporating too much air into the mixture.
4. Pour the Mixture Into the Mold:
   - Carefully pour the flan mixture over the cooled caramel in the cake pan or ramekins.
5. Bake the Flan:
   - Place the filled cake pan or ramekins into the preheated oven, setting them into the water bath.
   - Bake for 45-55 minutes for a large flan, or 30-40 minutes for individual ramekins, or until the flan is set around the edges but still slightly jiggly in the center.
6. Cool and Chill:
   - Once baked, remove the flan from the oven and let it cool to room temperature. Then, cover and refrigerate for at least 4 hours or overnight to chill and set completely.
7. Serve:
   - To serve, run a knife around the edges of the flan to loosen it from the mold. Place a serving plate on top of the mold and quickly invert it to release the flan onto the plate, allowing the caramel to flow over the top.
   - Slice and serve the flan chilled, garnished with fresh berries or mint leaves if desired.
8. Enjoy:
   - Enjoy the creamy and indulgent goodness of homemade flan!

This classic flan recipe yields a smooth and silky dessert with a perfect balance of sweetness. Feel free to customize it by adding a hint of citrus zest or a splash of liqueur to the flan mixture for extra flavor complexity.

Horchata

Ingredients:

- 1 cup long-grain white rice
- 4 cups water
- 1 cinnamon stick (or 1 teaspoon ground cinnamon)
- 1/2 cup granulated sugar (adjust to taste)
- 1 teaspoon vanilla extract
- 2 cups milk (or almond milk for a dairy-free version)
- Ground cinnamon, for garnish (optional)

Instructions:

1. Soak the Rice:
    - In a large bowl, combine the rice and 2 cups of water. Let it soak for at least 4 hours or overnight. This softens the rice and helps to extract its flavor.
2. Blend the Rice Mixture:
    - After soaking, pour the rice and water mixture into a blender. Add the cinnamon stick (or ground cinnamon), sugar, and vanilla extract. Blend on high speed for 2-3 minutes, or until the mixture is smooth and creamy.
3. Strain the Mixture:
    - Place a fine-mesh sieve or cheesecloth over a large bowl or pitcher. Pour the blended rice mixture through the sieve to strain out the rice solids, pressing down with a spoon or spatula to extract as much liquid as possible. Discard the rice solids.
4. Add Milk and Chill:
    - Stir in the milk (or almond milk) and the remaining 2 cups of water into the strained horchata mixture. Taste and adjust the sweetness by adding more sugar if desired.
    - Cover the pitcher or bowl and refrigerate the horchata for at least 1-2 hours, or until thoroughly chilled.
5. Serve:
    - Stir the horchata before serving to mix any settled ingredients. Pour the chilled horchata into glasses filled with ice cubes.
    - Garnish each glass with a sprinkle of ground cinnamon if desired.
6. Enjoy:

- Serve and enjoy the refreshing and creamy goodness of homemade horchata!

Horchata is best served cold and can be stored in the refrigerator for up to 3-4 days. Shake or stir before serving if any separation occurs. Adjust the sweetness and cinnamon flavor to suit your taste preferences.

Tostadas

Ingredients:

- Corn or flour tortillas (store-bought or homemade)
- Vegetable oil, for frying (if making fried tostadas)
- Salt, to taste

Instructions:

For Baked Tostadas:

1. Preheat the Oven:
    - Preheat your oven to 400°F (200°C).
2. Prepare the Tortillas:
    - Place the tortillas on a baking sheet lined with parchment paper or aluminum foil. Arrange them in a single layer, making sure they don't overlap.
3. Bake the Tortillas:
    - Bake the tortillas in the preheated oven for 5-7 minutes, or until they are crispy and lightly golden brown. Keep an eye on them to prevent burning.
4. Cool and Season:
    - Remove the baked tortillas from the oven and let them cool slightly on the baking sheet. Sprinkle with a pinch of salt to taste, if desired.

For Fried Tostadas:

1. Heat the Oil:
    - In a large skillet or frying pan, heat enough vegetable oil to cover the bottom of the pan over medium-high heat until hot but not smoking.
2. Fry the Tortillas:
    - Carefully place one tortilla in the hot oil and fry for about 1-2 minutes on each side, or until golden and crispy. Use kitchen tongs to flip the tortilla halfway through frying. Repeat with the remaining tortillas, frying one at a time or in batches as needed.
3. Drain and Cool:

- Once fried, transfer the tortillas to a plate lined with paper towels to drain off any excess oil. Let them cool slightly before serving.

Assemble the Tostadas:

1. Choose Your Toppings:
   - Once the tortillas are crispy and ready, it's time to add your favorite toppings. Common toppings include:
     - Refried beans
     - Shredded lettuce or cabbage
     - Cooked and seasoned meat (such as shredded chicken, beef, or pork)
     - Diced tomatoes
     - Sliced avocado or guacamole
     - Shredded cheese
     - Sour cream
     - Salsa or pico de gallo
     - Chopped cilantro
     - Sliced jalapeños
2. Layer the Toppings:
   - Spread a layer of refried beans onto each tostada shell, followed by your desired toppings. Get creative with the combinations and layering!
3. Serve and Enjoy:
   - Serve the tostadas immediately as an appetizer, snack, or main course. They're best enjoyed fresh while the tortillas are still crispy.
4. Customize:
   - Feel free to customize your tostadas with your favorite ingredients and toppings. You can make them vegetarian, vegan, or add protein-rich options like grilled shrimp or fish for a seafood twist.

Tostadas are a delicious and versatile dish that's easy to make at home. Whether you fry or bake the tortillas, the result is a crunchy base that pairs perfectly with a variety of toppings for a flavorful and satisfying meal.

Mole Poblano

Ingredients:

For the Mole Sauce:

- 3 tablespoons vegetable oil
- 3 ounces dried ancho chilies, stemmed and seeded
- 3 ounces dried pasilla chilies, stemmed and seeded
- 1 onion, chopped
- 4 cloves garlic, minced
- 1/2 cup almonds
- 1/4 cup raisins
- 1/4 cup sesame seeds
- 2 corn tortillas, torn into pieces
- 1/4 teaspoon ground cloves
- 1/4 teaspoon ground cinnamon
- 1/4 teaspoon ground coriander
- 1/4 teaspoon ground cumin
- 1/4 teaspoon dried oregano
- 1/4 teaspoon ground black pepper
- 1/4 teaspoon salt
- 3 cups chicken broth
- 1 ounce unsweetened chocolate
- 1 tablespoon sugar, or to taste

For Serving:

- Cooked chicken or turkey, shredded or cut into pieces
- Cooked rice
- Warm tortillas
- Sesame seeds, for garnish
- Chopped cilantro, for garnish

Instructions:

1. Prepare the Chilies:

- Heat a dry skillet over medium heat. Toast the dried ancho and pasilla chilies for 1-2 minutes on each side, until they become fragrant. Be careful not to burn them.
- Place the toasted chilies in a bowl and cover them with hot water. Let them soak for about 20-30 minutes, until they become softened.

2. Make the Mole Sauce:
    - In a large skillet or saucepan, heat the vegetable oil over medium heat. Add the chopped onion and minced garlic, and cook until softened and fragrant, about 5 minutes.
    - Add the almonds, raisins, and sesame seeds to the skillet, and cook for an additional 3-4 minutes, stirring frequently, until the nuts and seeds are lightly toasted.
    - Drain the soaked chilies and add them to the skillet along with the torn tortillas and spices (cloves, cinnamon, coriander, cumin, oregano, black pepper, and salt). Cook for another 2-3 minutes, stirring constantly, to toast the spices and soften the tortillas.
    - Transfer the mixture to a blender or food processor. Add the chicken broth and blend until smooth and well combined.
    - Return the mixture to the skillet or saucepan and bring it to a simmer over medium heat. Add the unsweetened chocolate and sugar, stirring until the chocolate is melted and the sauce is thickened. Taste and adjust the seasoning with more salt or sugar if needed.
3. Serve the Mole Poblano:
    - Serve the Mole Poblano over cooked chicken or turkey, accompanied by rice and warm tortillas.
    - Garnish with sesame seeds and chopped cilantro before serving.
4. Enjoy:
    - Enjoy the rich and complex flavors of homemade Mole Poblano!

This recipe yields a delicious and authentic Mole Poblano sauce that is sure to impress. It's worth the effort to make from scratch, and the leftovers can be stored in the refrigerator for several days or frozen for longer storage.

Barbacoa

Ingredients:

For the Barbacoa:

- 3 pounds beef chuck roast or beef brisket, trimmed of excess fat
- 1 onion, chopped
- 4 cloves garlic, minced
- 2 chipotle peppers in adobo sauce, chopped
- 2 tablespoons adobo sauce (from the chipotle pepper can)
- 1/4 cup lime juice
- 2 tablespoons apple cider vinegar
- 2 teaspoons ground cumin
- 2 teaspoons dried oregano
- 2 teaspoons smoked paprika
- 1 teaspoon ground coriander
- 1 teaspoon salt
- 1/2 teaspoon black pepper
- 1 cup beef broth or water

For Serving:

- Tortillas, for tacos or burritos
- Chopped cilantro
- Diced onions
- Lime wedges
- Sliced avocado
- Salsa or pico de gallo
- Sour cream or Mexican crema

Instructions:

1. Prepare the Beef:
    - Cut the beef chuck roast or brisket into large chunks, about 2 inches in size. This will help the meat cook evenly and absorb the flavors of the marinade.

2. Make the Marinade:
   - In a blender or food processor, combine the chopped onion, minced garlic, chipotle peppers, adobo sauce, lime juice, apple cider vinegar, ground cumin, dried oregano, smoked paprika, ground coriander, salt, and black pepper. Blend until smooth.
3. Marinate the Beef:
   - Place the beef chunks in a large bowl or resealable plastic bag. Pour the marinade over the beef, making sure it's well coated. Cover the bowl or seal the bag, and refrigerate for at least 4 hours or overnight to marinate and allow the flavors to penetrate the meat.
4. Slow Cook the Barbacoa:
   - Once the beef has marinated, transfer it along with the marinade to a slow cooker. Add the beef broth or water to the slow cooker, ensuring that the beef is submerged in liquid.
   - Cover and cook on low heat for 6-8 hours, or until the beef is tender and easily shreds with a fork.
5. Shred the Beef:
   - Once the beef is cooked, use two forks to shred it into bite-sized pieces directly in the slow cooker. Mix the shredded beef with the cooking liquid and spices to ensure it's evenly coated.
6. Serve the Barbacoa:
   - Serve the shredded beef barbacoa warm with tortillas and your favorite toppings such as chopped cilantro, diced onions, lime wedges, sliced avocado, salsa, or sour cream.
   - Enjoy the flavorful and tender beef barbacoa in tacos, burritos, or as a main dish with rice and beans!

This homemade beef barbacoa recipe is easy to make and yields tender and flavorful meat that's perfect for feeding a crowd or enjoying as leftovers throughout the week. Adjust the spice level to your preference by adding more or fewer chipotle peppers and adobo sauce.

Sopes

Ingredients:

For the Sopes:

- 2 cups masa harina (corn flour)
- 1 1/4 cups warm water
- 1/2 teaspoon salt
- Vegetable oil, for frying

For Topping (suggested):

- Refried beans
- Cooked and seasoned meat (such as shredded chicken, beef, or pork)
- Chopped lettuce or cabbage
- Diced tomatoes
- Sliced avocado or guacamole
- Crumbled queso fresco or shredded cheese
- Mexican crema or sour cream
- Salsa or pico de gallo
- Chopped cilantro

Instructions:

1. Prepare the Dough:
    - In a large mixing bowl, combine the masa harina and salt. Gradually add the warm water, mixing with your hands until a soft and pliable dough forms. If the dough is too dry, add a little more water, one tablespoon at a time. If it's too sticky, add a little more masa harina.
2. Form the Sopes:
    - Pinch off a golf ball-sized portion of dough and roll it into a smooth ball. Flatten the ball between your palms to form a thick disc, about 1/4 to 1/2 inch thick. Use your fingers to pinch and form a raised edge around the circumference of the disc, creating a shallow well in the center. Repeat with the remaining dough.
3. Cook the Sopes:

- Heat a non-stick skillet or griddle over medium heat. Lightly grease the skillet with vegetable oil.
- Place the formed sopes on the hot skillet and cook for 2-3 minutes on each side, or until lightly golden brown and cooked through. Press down gently with a spatula while cooking to ensure even cooking and to help them keep their shape.

4. Fry the Sopes (optional):
   - Alternatively, you can fry the formed sopes in hot vegetable oil until golden brown and crispy on both sides. Drain on paper towels to remove excess oil.
5. Assemble the Sopes:
   - Once the sopes are cooked, top each one with a spoonful of refried beans, followed by your choice of cooked and seasoned meat, chopped lettuce or cabbage, diced tomatoes, sliced avocado or guacamole, crumbled queso fresco or shredded cheese, Mexican crema or sour cream, salsa or pico de gallo, and chopped cilantro.
6. Serve:
   - Serve the sopes immediately, while still warm, as an appetizer, snack, or light meal. Enjoy the delicious combination of flavors and textures!

Sopes are highly customizable, so feel free to experiment with different toppings and combinations to suit your taste preferences. They're a fun and satisfying dish to make at home and perfect for sharing with family and friends.

Pico de Gallo

Ingredients:

- 4 medium ripe tomatoes, diced
- 1/2 onion, finely chopped
- 1/4 cup fresh cilantro, chopped
- 1-2 jalapeño or serrano peppers, seeded and finely chopped (adjust to taste)
- 2 tablespoons fresh lime juice (about 1 lime)
- Salt, to taste

Instructions:

1. Prepare the Ingredients:
   - Wash and dry the tomatoes, cilantro, and peppers. Remove the stems from the tomatoes and cut them into small dice. Finely chop the onion, cilantro, and jalapeño or serrano peppers. For a milder salsa, remove the seeds and membranes from the peppers before chopping.
2. Combine the Ingredients:
   - In a medium-sized bowl, combine the diced tomatoes, chopped onion, cilantro, and chopped peppers.
3. Add Lime Juice and Salt:
   - Squeeze fresh lime juice over the tomato mixture. Start with about 1 tablespoon of lime juice and add more to taste, depending on your preference for acidity.
   - Season the pico de gallo with salt, starting with a small amount and adding more as needed to enhance the flavors. Mix well to combine.
4. Chill (optional):
   - For best flavor, let the pico de gallo chill in the refrigerator for at least 30 minutes before serving. This allows the flavors to meld together and develop.
5. Serve:
   - Serve the pico de gallo as a dip with tortilla chips, or use it as a topping for tacos, burritos, grilled meats, seafood, or any dish that could benefit from a fresh and zesty salsa.
6. Enjoy:
   - Enjoy the delicious and vibrant flavors of homemade pico de gallo!

Feel free to customize the pico de gallo to suit your taste preferences. You can adjust the amount of onion, cilantro, and peppers, or add additional ingredients such as diced avocado, minced garlic, or chopped mango for a unique twist. Experiment with different varieties of tomatoes and peppers for variations in flavor and heat level.

Chiles en Nogada

Ingredients:

For the Filling:

- 6 large poblano peppers
- 1 pound ground beef or pork
- 1 onion, finely chopped
- 2 cloves garlic, minced
- 1/2 cup diced tomatoes
- 1/2 cup diced apple
- 1/2 cup diced pear
- 1/4 cup raisins
- 1/4 cup sliced almonds
- 1/4 cup chopped walnuts
- 1/4 cup chopped fresh parsley
- 1 teaspoon ground cinnamon
- 1/2 teaspoon ground cloves
- Salt and pepper, to taste

For the Walnut Sauce (Nogada):

- 1 cup walnuts, soaked in water for 1 hour
- 1 cup milk
- 1/2 cup Mexican crema or sour cream
- 1/4 cup queso fresco or mild goat cheese
- 1/4 cup sugar
- 1/4 teaspoon ground cinnamon
- Salt, to taste

For Garnish:

- Pomegranate seeds
- Chopped fresh parsley

Instructions:

1. Prepare the Poblano Peppers:
   - Roast the poblano peppers over an open flame or under the broiler until the skins are charred and blistered on all sides. Place the roasted peppers in a plastic bag or covered bowl and let them steam for about 10 minutes. This will make it easier to peel off the skins. Once cooled, peel off the skins, make a slit down one side of each pepper, and carefully remove the seeds and membranes.
2. Make the Filling:
   - In a large skillet, cook the ground meat over medium heat until browned. Add the chopped onion and garlic, and cook until softened.
   - Stir in the diced tomatoes, apple, pear, raisins, almonds, walnuts, parsley, ground cinnamon, ground cloves, salt, and pepper. Cook for an additional 5-7 minutes, or until the mixture is well combined and the fruits are tender. Remove from heat and let cool slightly.
3. Stuff the Peppers:
   - Carefully stuff each poblano pepper with the meat and fruit mixture, making sure not to overfill them. Gently press the edges of the peppers together to seal the filling inside.
4. Make the Walnut Sauce (Nogada):
   - In a blender or food processor, combine the soaked walnuts, milk, Mexican crema or sour cream, queso fresco or mild goat cheese, sugar, ground cinnamon, and salt. Blend until smooth and creamy. If the sauce is too thick, you can add a little more milk to reach your desired consistency.
5. Assemble the Dish:
   - Place the stuffed poblano peppers on a serving platter. Spoon the walnut sauce over the top of each pepper, covering them generously.
   - Garnish the chiles en nogada with pomegranate seeds and chopped fresh parsley.
6. Serve:
   - Serve the chiles en nogada immediately, while still warm, as a festive and flavorful main dish.

Chiles en nogada is a labor of love, but the end result is well worth the effort. It's a dish that is rich in flavor and history, making it a special treat for any occasion.

Enchiladas Suizas

Ingredients:

For the Enchiladas:

- 12 corn tortillas
- 2 cups cooked shredded chicken (rotisserie chicken works well)
- 1 cup shredded Monterey Jack cheese or Swiss cheese
- 1/2 cup chopped white onion
- 1/4 cup chopped fresh cilantro

For the Green Sauce:

- 3 cups tomatillos, husked and rinsed
- 1/2 onion, quartered
- 2 cloves garlic
- 1-2 jalapeño peppers, seeded (adjust to taste)
- 1/2 cup fresh cilantro leaves
- 1/2 cup Mexican crema or sour cream
- Salt, to taste

For Garnish:

- Mexican crema or sour cream
- Sliced avocado
- Fresh cilantro leaves
- Sliced radishes
- Lime wedges

Instructions:

1. Prepare the Green Sauce:
    - In a medium saucepan, combine the tomatillos, quartered onion, garlic cloves, and jalapeño peppers. Cover with water and bring to a boil over high heat. Reduce the heat to medium-low and simmer for about 10-15 minutes, or until the tomatillos are tender.

- Using a slotted spoon, transfer the cooked vegetables to a blender or food processor. Add the cilantro leaves and Mexican crema or sour cream. Blend until smooth. Season with salt to taste. Set aside.
2. Preheat the Oven:
    - Preheat your oven to 350°F (175°C).
3. Assemble the Enchiladas:
    - Warm the corn tortillas in the microwave for a few seconds or on a skillet for a few seconds on each side until soft and pliable.
    - Spread a small amount of the green sauce on the bottom of a 9x13-inch baking dish.
    - Place a spoonful of shredded chicken down the center of each tortilla. Roll up the tortillas and place them seam side down in the baking dish.
    - Pour the remaining green sauce over the top of the rolled enchiladas, covering them evenly.
    - Sprinkle the shredded cheese over the top of the sauce-covered enchiladas.
4. Bake the Enchiladas:
    - Cover the baking dish with aluminum foil and bake in the preheated oven for 20-25 minutes, or until the cheese is melted and bubbly.
5. Serve:
    - Remove the foil from the baking dish. Garnish the enchiladas with chopped onion and cilantro.
    - Serve the Enchiladas Suizas hot, garnished with Mexican crema or sour cream, sliced avocado, fresh cilantro leaves, sliced radishes, and lime wedges on the side.

Enchiladas Suizas are delicious served with rice and beans, or a simple salad for a complete meal. Enjoy the creamy, flavorful goodness of this classic Mexican dish!

Churros

Ingredients:

For the Churro Dough:

- 1 cup water
- 2 tablespoons white sugar
- 1/2 teaspoon salt
- 2 tablespoons vegetable oil
- 1 cup all-purpose flour

For Frying and Coating:

- Vegetable oil, for frying
- 1/4 cup white sugar
- 1 teaspoon ground cinnamon

For Chocolate Dipping Sauce (optional):

- 1/2 cup semisweet chocolate chips
- 1/2 cup heavy cream
- 1/2 teaspoon vanilla extract

Instructions:

1. Make the Churro Dough:
    - In a medium saucepan, combine water, sugar, salt, and vegetable oil. Bring to a boil over medium-high heat.
    - Remove from heat and add the flour all at once. Stir quickly with a wooden spoon until the mixture forms a ball of dough and pulls away from the sides of the pan.
    - Let the dough cool for a few minutes.
2. Fry the Churros:
    - Heat vegetable oil in a deep fryer or a large, heavy-bottomed pot to 375°F (190°C).

- Transfer the dough to a piping bag fitted with a large star tip. Pipe strips of dough directly into the hot oil, using scissors or a knife to cut them to your desired length. Fry 3-4 churros at a time, depending on the size of your fryer or pot, being careful not to overcrowd.
- Fry the churros until they are golden brown and crispy, about 3-4 minutes, turning them occasionally for even cooking.
- Remove the fried churros from the oil using a slotted spoon and transfer them to a paper towel-lined plate to drain any excess oil.

3. Coat the Churros:
    - In a shallow dish, combine the white sugar and ground cinnamon. Roll the warm churros in the cinnamon sugar mixture until they are evenly coated.
4. Make the Chocolate Dipping Sauce (optional):
    - In a small saucepan, heat the heavy cream over medium heat until it just begins to simmer.
    - Remove from heat and add the chocolate chips and vanilla extract. Let the mixture sit for 1-2 minutes, then stir until the chocolate is completely melted and the sauce is smooth.
5. Serve:
    - Serve the freshly fried and coated churros immediately, with the warm chocolate dipping sauce on the side if desired.

Enjoy these homemade churros as a delicious and indulgent treat! They're best enjoyed fresh and warm, so be sure to devour them soon after frying.

Cochinita Pibil

Ingredients:

For the Marinade:

- 3-4 pounds pork shoulder or pork butt, cut into large chunks
- 1/2 cup bitter orange juice (or substitute with equal parts orange juice and lime juice)
- 1/4 cup lime juice
- 1/4 cup white vinegar
- 3 tablespoons achiote paste
- 4 cloves garlic, minced
- 1 teaspoon ground cumin
- 1 teaspoon dried oregano
- 1 teaspoon salt
- 1/2 teaspoon black pepper

For Cooking:

- Banana leaves (optional, for wrapping)
- 1 onion, thinly sliced
- 2-3 bay leaves
- 1/2 cup chicken broth or water

For Serving:

- Corn tortillas
- Pickled red onions (optional)
- Sliced avocado
- Fresh cilantro leaves
- Lime wedges

Instructions:

1. Prepare the Marinade:

- In a blender or food processor, combine the bitter orange juice, lime juice, white vinegar, achiote paste, minced garlic, ground cumin, dried oregano, salt, and black pepper. Blend until smooth.

2. Marinate the Pork:
    - Place the pork chunks in a large bowl or resealable plastic bag. Pour the marinade over the pork, making sure it's well coated. Cover the bowl or seal the bag, and refrigerate for at least 4 hours or overnight to marinate and allow the flavors to penetrate the meat.
3. Preheat the Oven:
    - Preheat your oven to 325°F (160°C).
4. Assemble and Cook the Cochinita Pibil:
    - If using banana leaves, briefly heat them over an open flame or in a hot skillet to soften them.
    - Place the sliced onions and bay leaves in the bottom of a large roasting pan or Dutch oven.
    - Arrange the marinated pork chunks on top of the onions and bay leaves. Pour the chicken broth or water over the pork.
    - If using banana leaves, wrap the pork tightly in the leaves, folding them around the meat to form a packet. If not using banana leaves, cover the roasting pan or Dutch oven tightly with aluminum foil.
    - Place the roasting pan or Dutch oven in the preheated oven and roast for 3-4 hours, or until the pork is tender and easily shreds with a fork.
5. Serve:
    - Remove the cochinita pibil from the oven and let it cool slightly. Use two forks to shred the pork into bite-sized pieces.
    - Serve the cochinita pibil warm, wrapped in warm corn tortillas and topped with pickled red onions (if using), sliced avocado, fresh cilantro leaves, and lime wedges on the side.

Cochinita pibil is a flavorful and aromatic dish that's perfect for sharing with family and friends. Enjoy the tender and succulent pork with the vibrant and tangy flavors of the marinade!

Molletes

Ingredients:

- 4 bolillo rolls or French bread rolls, sliced in half lengthwise
- 1 can (15 ounces) refried beans
- 1 cup shredded cheese (such as Oaxaca cheese, Monterey Jack, or Cheddar)
- Salsa, for serving (optional)
- Sliced avocado, for serving (optional)
- Chopped cilantro, for serving (optional)

Instructions:

1. Preheat the Oven:
    - Preheat your oven to 350°F (175°C).
2. Prepare the Bread:
    - Place the bolillo or French bread halves cut-side up on a baking sheet.
3. Toast the Bread:
    - Place the baking sheet in the preheated oven and toast the bread halves until they are lightly golden and crispy around the edges, about 5-7 minutes.
4. Warm the Refried Beans:
    - While the bread is toasting, heat the refried beans in a small saucepan over medium heat until warmed through. You can add a splash of water or chicken broth to thin them out if needed.
5. Assemble the Molletes:
    - Once the bread is toasted, spread a generous amount of warmed refried beans over each bread half.
    - Sprinkle shredded cheese evenly over the top of the refried beans.
6. Bake the Molletes:
    - Return the baking sheet to the oven and bake the molletes for an additional 5-7 minutes, or until the cheese is melted and bubbly.
7. Serve:
    - Remove the molletes from the oven and let them cool slightly.
    - Serve the molletes warm, garnished with salsa, sliced avocado, chopped cilantro, or any other toppings of your choice.

Molletes are best enjoyed fresh out of the oven when the cheese is still gooey and melted. They make a delicious and comforting dish that's perfect for any time of day!

Cactus Salad (Ensalada de Nopales)

Ingredients:

- 4 nopales pads (prickly pear cactus pads)
- 1 tablespoon olive oil
- 1/2 small red onion, thinly sliced
- 2 tomatoes, diced
- 1/4 cup chopped cilantro
- 1 jalapeño or serrano pepper, seeded and finely chopped (optional)
- Juice of 1 lime
- Salt and pepper, to taste
- Crumbled queso fresco or cotija cheese, for garnish (optional)
- Avocado slices, for garnish (optional)

Instructions:

1. Prepare the Nopales:
    - Using a pair of tongs, hold each nopales pad over an open flame or place them on a hot grill. Cook for a few minutes on each side until they are slightly charred and the spines are no longer visible. Be careful not to overcook, as nopales can become slimy if overdone.
    - Once cooked, remove the nopales pads from the heat and let them cool. Use a sharp knife to scrape off any remaining spines and cut the pads into bite-sized pieces.
2. Cook the Nopales:
    - Heat olive oil in a skillet over medium heat. Add the sliced red onion and cook until softened and slightly caramelized, about 3-4 minutes.
    - Add the diced nopales to the skillet and cook for an additional 5-7 minutes, stirring occasionally, until they are tender and lightly browned.
    - Remove the skillet from the heat and let the nopales cool to room temperature.
3. Assemble the Salad:
    - In a large bowl, combine the cooked nopales and onions with the diced tomatoes, chopped cilantro, and finely chopped jalapeño or serrano pepper (if using).
    - Squeeze the lime juice over the salad and toss gently to combine. Season with salt and pepper to taste.
4. Garnish and Serve:

- Transfer the ensalada de nopales to a serving platter or individual plates.
- If desired, garnish the salad with crumbled queso fresco or cotija cheese and slices of avocado.
- Serve the cactus salad immediately as a refreshing side dish or as a topping for tacos, tostadas, or alongside grilled meats.

Ensalada de nopales is best enjoyed fresh, and it makes a delicious and healthy addition to any Mexican-inspired meal!

Mexican Street Corn (Elote)

Ingredients:

- 4 ears of corn, husked
- 1/4 cup mayonnaise
- 1/4 cup sour cream or Mexican crema
- 1/2 cup crumbled cotija cheese or feta cheese
- 1 teaspoon chili powder (or to taste)
- 1/4 cup chopped fresh cilantro (optional)
- Lime wedges, for serving

Instructions:

1. Grill or Boil the Corn:
    - Preheat your grill to medium-high heat. Alternatively, you can boil the corn in a large pot of water.
    - Grill or boil the corn for about 8-10 minutes, or until it's tender and lightly charred in spots. Turn the corn occasionally for even cooking.
2. Prepare the Sauce:
    - In a small bowl, mix together the mayonnaise and sour cream until well combined.
3. Assemble the Elote:
    - Once the corn is cooked, brush each ear of corn with the mayonnaise and sour cream mixture, coating it evenly on all sides.
    - Sprinkle the crumbled cotija cheese or feta cheese over the corn, followed by the chili powder.
    - Garnish with chopped fresh cilantro, if desired.
4. Serve:
    - Serve the Mexican street corn immediately, while it's still warm, with lime wedges on the side.
    - Squeeze lime juice over the corn just before eating for an extra burst of flavor.

Mexican street corn is a delicious and satisfying snack or side dish that's perfect for summer barbecues, picnics, or any time you're craving a taste of Mexico!

Empanadas

Ingredients:

For the Dough:

- 3 cups all-purpose flour
- 1 teaspoon salt
- 1/2 cup cold unsalted butter, cut into small cubes
- 1 large egg
- 1/2 cup cold water

For the Beef Filling:

- 1 tablespoon olive oil
- 1 onion, finely chopped
- 2 cloves garlic, minced
- 1 pound ground beef
- 1 teaspoon ground cumin
- 1 teaspoon paprika
- 1/2 teaspoon chili powder (optional)
- Salt and pepper, to taste
- 1/4 cup chopped fresh cilantro (optional)
- 1/4 cup pitted green olives, chopped (optional)
- 2 hard-boiled eggs, chopped (optional)

For Assembly:

- 1 egg, beaten (for egg wash)
- Additional flour, for rolling out the dough

Instructions:

1. Make the Dough:

- In a large mixing bowl, combine the flour and salt. Add the cold cubed butter and use your fingers or a pastry cutter to cut the butter into the flour until the mixture resembles coarse crumbs.
- In a small bowl, beat the egg with the cold water. Gradually add the egg mixture to the flour mixture, stirring until a dough forms.
- Turn the dough out onto a lightly floured surface and knead gently until smooth. Wrap the dough in plastic wrap and refrigerate for at least 30 minutes, or up to 1 hour.

2. Prepare the Beef Filling:
   - In a skillet, heat the olive oil over medium heat. Add the chopped onion and garlic, and cook until softened and translucent.
   - Add the ground beef to the skillet and cook, breaking it apart with a spoon, until browned and cooked through.
   - Stir in the ground cumin, paprika, chili powder (if using), salt, and pepper. Cook for an additional 2-3 minutes to allow the flavors to meld.
   - Remove the skillet from the heat and stir in the chopped cilantro, chopped olives, and chopped hard-boiled eggs (if using). Set aside to cool.

3. Assemble the Empanadas:
   - Preheat your oven to 375°F (190°C). Line a baking sheet with parchment paper.
   - On a lightly floured surface, roll out the chilled dough to about 1/8 inch thickness. Use a round cutter or a small bowl to cut out circles of dough, about 4-5 inches in diameter.
   - Spoon a small amount of the beef filling onto one half of each dough circle, leaving a border around the edges. Fold the other half of the dough over the filling to create a half-moon shape. Press the edges together to seal, then crimp with a fork to secure.
   - Place the assembled empanadas on the prepared baking sheet. Brush the tops with beaten egg for a shiny finish.

4. Bake the Empanadas:
   - Bake the empanadas in the preheated oven for 20-25 minutes, or until golden brown and crispy.

5. Serve:
   - Allow the empanadas to cool slightly before serving. Enjoy them warm as a delicious snack or meal, either on their own or with your favorite dipping sauce.

Feel free to customize the filling with your favorite ingredients or spices, and experiment with different shapes and sizes for the empanadas. They're versatile, portable, and perfect for any occasion!

Picadillo

Ingredients:

- 1 tablespoon olive oil
- 1 onion, finely chopped
- 2 cloves garlic, minced
- 1 pound ground beef
- 1 bell pepper, diced
- 1 tomato, diced
- 1/4 cup raisins
- 1/4 cup green olives, sliced
- 2 tablespoons tomato paste
- 1 teaspoon ground cumin
- 1 teaspoon dried oregano
- 1/2 teaspoon paprika
- Salt and pepper, to taste
- 1/2 cup beef broth or water
- Cooked white rice, for serving
- Chopped fresh cilantro or parsley, for garnish (optional)

Instructions:

1. Cook the Aromatics:
    - Heat the olive oil in a large skillet or frying pan over medium heat. Add the chopped onion and minced garlic, and cook until softened and fragrant, about 2-3 minutes.
2. Brown the Ground Beef:
    - Add the ground beef to the skillet, breaking it apart with a spoon, and cook until browned and no longer pink, stirring occasionally.
3. Add the Vegetables and Seasonings:
    - Stir in the diced bell pepper and tomato, along with the raisins, sliced green olives, tomato paste, ground cumin, dried oregano, paprika, salt, and pepper. Cook for an additional 3-4 minutes, until the vegetables are slightly softened and the spices are fragrant.
4. Simmer the Picadillo:
    - Pour the beef broth or water into the skillet and stir to combine, scraping up any browned bits from the bottom of the pan. Bring the mixture to a simmer, then reduce the heat to low. Cover and let the picadillo simmer

gently for 15-20 minutes, stirring occasionally, to allow the flavors to meld and the sauce to thicken slightly.
5. Serve:
    - Serve the picadillo hot over cooked white rice, garnished with chopped fresh cilantro or parsley if desired.

Picadillo is a comforting and flavorful dish that's perfect for a satisfying meal any day of the week. Feel free to customize the recipe by adding your favorite vegetables or spices, and enjoy the delicious taste of this classic Latin American dish!

Tamale Pie

Ingredients:

For the filling:

- 1 lb (450g) ground beef or turkey
- 1 onion, diced
- 1 bell pepper, diced
- 2 cloves garlic, minced
- 1 can (14 oz/400g) diced tomatoes, drained
- 1 can (14 oz/400g) black beans, drained and rinsed (optional)
- 1 cup (240ml) corn kernels (fresh, canned, or frozen)
- 1 tablespoon chili powder
- 1 teaspoon ground cumin
- Salt and pepper to taste
- 1 cup (120g) shredded cheese (cheddar, Monterey Jack, or a blend)

For the cornmeal topping:

- 1 cup (120g) cornmeal
- 1 cup (240ml) chicken or vegetable broth
- 1 cup (240ml) milk
- 1 tablespoon butter
- Salt to taste

Instructions:

1. Preheat your oven to 375°F (190°C). Grease a 9x13-inch baking dish.
2. In a large skillet, cook the ground beef or turkey over medium heat until browned. Drain any excess fat.
3. Add the diced onion and bell pepper to the skillet and cook until softened, about 5 minutes. Stir in the minced garlic and cook for another minute.

4. Add the diced tomatoes, black beans (if using), corn kernels, chili powder, cumin, salt, and pepper to the skillet. Stir well to combine. Let the mixture simmer for about 5 minutes, allowing the flavors to meld together. Remove from heat.
5. Transfer the meat mixture to the prepared baking dish and spread it out evenly. Sprinkle the shredded cheese over the top.
6. In a medium saucepan, bring the chicken or vegetable broth and milk to a simmer over medium heat. Gradually whisk in the cornmeal, stirring constantly to prevent lumps from forming. Cook until the mixture thickens, about 5 minutes.
7. Remove the saucepan from heat and stir in the butter and salt until the butter is melted and the mixture is smooth.
8. Pour the cornmeal mixture over the meat filling in the baking dish, spreading it out evenly to cover the filling completely.
9. Bake in the preheated oven for 25-30 minutes, or until the cornmeal topping is golden and set.
10. Let the tamale pie cool for a few minutes before serving. Garnish with chopped cilantro, sliced jalapeños, or a dollop of sour cream if desired. Enjoy your delicious tamale pie!

Mexican Hot Chocolate

Ingredients:

- 2 cups (480ml) milk (whole milk or any milk of your choice)
- 2 ounces (about 60g) dark chocolate, chopped (preferably Mexican chocolate if available)
- 2 tablespoons granulated sugar (adjust to taste)
- 1/2 teaspoon ground cinnamon
- Pinch of chili powder or cayenne pepper (optional, for a hint of heat)
- Pinch of salt
- 1/2 teaspoon vanilla extract (optional)
- Whipped cream, for serving (optional)
- Ground cinnamon or cocoa powder, for garnish (optional)

Instructions:

1. In a saucepan, heat the milk over medium heat until it starts to steam, but not boil.
2. Add the chopped dark chocolate to the saucepan and whisk continuously until the chocolate is completely melted and the mixture is smooth.
3. Stir in the granulated sugar, ground cinnamon, chili powder or cayenne pepper (if using), and a pinch of salt. Continue to whisk until the sugar is dissolved and the spices are well incorporated.
4. Taste the hot chocolate and adjust the sweetness or spiciness according to your preference. You can add more sugar or spices if desired.
5. If using, stir in the vanilla extract for added flavor.
6. Once everything is well combined and heated through, remove the saucepan from the heat.
7. Pour the Mexican hot chocolate into mugs and serve hot.
8. Optionally, top each mug with a dollop of whipped cream and sprinkle with ground cinnamon or cocoa powder for garnish.
9. Enjoy your delicious and comforting Mexican hot chocolate!

Feel free to adjust the ingredients and spices according to your taste preferences. Some variations include adding a dash of nutmeg or using sweetened condensed milk for extra richness.

Tinga de Pollo

Ingredients:

- 2 lbs (about 900g) boneless, skinless chicken breasts or thighs
- 2 tablespoons vegetable oil
- 1 onion, thinly sliced
- 2 cloves garlic, minced
- 2 chipotle peppers in adobo sauce, finely chopped (adjust to taste)
- 1 can (14 oz/400g) diced tomatoes
- 1 teaspoon dried oregano
- 1 teaspoon ground cumin
- Salt and pepper to taste
- 1/2 cup (120ml) chicken broth or water
- Corn or flour tortillas, for serving
- Optional toppings: chopped cilantro, diced onion, crumbled queso fresco, avocado slices, lime wedges

Instructions:

1. In a large pot or Dutch oven, heat the vegetable oil over medium-high heat. Add the sliced onion and cook until softened and lightly browned, about 5 minutes.
2. Stir in the minced garlic and chopped chipotle peppers. Cook for another minute until fragrant.
3. Add the diced tomatoes (with their juices) to the pot, along with the dried oregano, ground cumin, salt, and pepper. Stir well to combine.
4. Nestle the chicken breasts or thighs into the tomato mixture, making sure they are submerged in the sauce.
5. Pour the chicken broth or water over the chicken to cover it slightly.
6. Bring the mixture to a simmer, then reduce the heat to low. Cover the pot and let it simmer gently for about 20-25 minutes, or until the chicken is cooked through and tender.
7. Once the chicken is cooked, remove it from the pot and transfer it to a cutting board. Use two forks to shred the chicken into bite-sized pieces.
8. Return the shredded chicken to the pot with the tomato sauce. Stir well to coat the chicken evenly with the sauce.
9. Continue to simmer the tinga for another 5-10 minutes, allowing the flavors to meld together and the sauce to thicken slightly.
10. Taste the tinga and adjust the seasoning with salt and pepper if needed.
11. Serve the tinga de pollo hot, spooned onto warm tortillas or over rice. Garnish with your choice of toppings such as chopped cilantro, diced onion, crumbled queso fresco, avocado slices, and lime wedges.

Enjoy your homemade Tinga de Pollo!

Mexican Wedding Cookies (Polvorones)

Ingredients:

- 1 cup (2 sticks or 226g) unsalted butter, softened
- 1/2 cup (60g) powdered sugar, plus more for coating
- 1 teaspoon vanilla extract
- 2 cups (240g) all-purpose flour
- 1 cup (120g) finely chopped nuts (such as pecans, walnuts, or almonds)

Instructions:

1. Preheat your oven to 350°F (175°C). Line a baking sheet with parchment paper or lightly grease it.
2. In a large mixing bowl, cream together the softened butter and powdered sugar until light and fluffy.
3. Stir in the vanilla extract until well combined.
4. Gradually add the flour to the butter mixture, mixing until a dough forms. Fold in the chopped nuts until evenly distributed throughout the dough.
5. Shape the dough into small balls, about 1 inch (2.5 cm) in diameter, and place them on the prepared baking sheet, spacing them a few inches apart.
6. Bake the cookies in the preheated oven for 12-15 minutes, or until they are set and just starting to turn golden brown on the bottom.
7. Remove the cookies from the oven and let them cool on the baking sheet for a few minutes.
8. While the cookies are still warm, gently roll them in powdered sugar until they are coated completely. You can also dust them with additional powdered sugar using a sifter or fine mesh sieve.
9. Transfer the coated cookies to a wire rack to cool completely.
10. Once cooled, roll the cookies in powdered sugar again for a second coating, if desired, to achieve a snowy appearance.
11. Store the Mexican Wedding Cookies in an airtight container at room temperature for up to a week. They also freeze well for longer storage.

Enjoy these buttery, nutty delights as a sweet treat for weddings, holidays, or any special occasion!

Tlayudas

Ingredients:

For the Tlayudas:

- Large corn tortillas (you can also use store-bought tostadas)
- Refried beans (homemade or canned)
- Oaxacan cheese or shredded mozzarella cheese
- Optional toppings: sliced avocado, shredded lettuce, diced tomatoes, thinly sliced onions, cooked and shredded chicken or beef, chorizo, salsa, cilantro, lime wedges

Instructions:

1. Preheat a grill, grill pan, or large skillet over medium-high heat.
2. Place a tortilla on the grill or skillet and cook for about 1-2 minutes on each side, until it is lightly toasted and crispy. Repeat with the remaining tortillas.
3. Once the tortillas are toasted, spread a layer of refried beans evenly over each tortilla.
4. Sprinkle a generous amount of Oaxacan cheese or shredded mozzarella cheese over the refried beans.
5. If desired, add any additional toppings of your choice, such as sliced avocado, shredded lettuce, diced tomatoes, thinly sliced onions, cooked and shredded chicken or beef, chorizo, salsa, or cilantro.
6. Place the topped tortillas back on the grill or skillet and cook for another 2-3 minutes, or until the cheese is melted and bubbly.
7. Remove the Tlayudas from the grill or skillet and transfer them to serving plates.
8. Serve the Tlayudas hot, accompanied by lime wedges for squeezing over the top.

Enjoy these crispy and flavorful Tlayudas as a delicious and satisfying meal or snack! They're perfect for sharing with friends and family, especially during outdoor gatherings or casual dinners.

Tres Leches Cake

Ingredients:

For the cake:

- 1 cup (125g) all-purpose flour
- 1 1/2 teaspoons baking powder
- 1/4 teaspoon salt
- 5 large eggs, separated
- 1 cup (200g) granulated sugar, divided
- 1/3 cup (80ml) whole milk
- 1 teaspoon vanilla extract

For the tres leches mixture:

- 1 can (12 oz/354ml) evaporated milk
- 1 can (14 oz/397g) sweetened condensed milk
- 1 cup (240ml) heavy cream

For the topping (optional):

- Whipped cream
- Maraschino cherries or fresh fruit for garnish

Instructions:

1. Preheat your oven to 350°F (175°C). Grease and flour a 9x13-inch baking dish.
2. In a medium bowl, sift together the flour, baking powder, and salt. Set aside.
3. In a large mixing bowl, beat the egg yolks with 3/4 cup of granulated sugar until pale and fluffy. Stir in the milk and vanilla extract.
4. Gradually fold in the dry ingredients until just combined.

5. In a separate clean mixing bowl, beat the egg whites until soft peaks form. Gradually add the remaining 1/4 cup of granulated sugar and continue to beat until stiff peaks form.
6. Gently fold the beaten egg whites into the batter until no streaks remain.
7. Pour the batter into the prepared baking dish and spread it out evenly.
8. Bake in the preheated oven for 25-30 minutes, or until a toothpick inserted into the center comes out clean.
9. While the cake is baking, prepare the tres leches mixture. In a mixing bowl, whisk together the evaporated milk, sweetened condensed milk, and heavy cream until well combined. Set aside.
10. Once the cake is done baking, remove it from the oven and let it cool slightly in the pan for about 10 minutes.
11. Using a fork or skewer, poke holes all over the surface of the cake.
12. Slowly pour the tres leches mixture evenly over the warm cake, allowing it to absorb the liquid.
13. Cover the cake and refrigerate for at least 4 hours or overnight to allow the flavors to meld and the cake to absorb the milks.
14. Before serving, you can optionally top the cake with whipped cream and garnish with maraschino cherries or fresh fruit.
15. Slice and serve the Tres Leches Cake cold. Enjoy the rich and creamy goodness of this classic dessert!

Tres Leches Cake is perfect for celebrations or any time you want to indulge in a sweet and satisfying treat.

Camarones a la Diabla

Ingredients:

- 1 lb (about 450g) large shrimp, peeled and deveined
- 3 tablespoons vegetable oil
- 1 onion, finely chopped
- 3 cloves garlic, minced
- 2 cups (500ml) tomato puree or crushed tomatoes
- 2-3 chipotle peppers in adobo sauce, chopped (adjust to taste)
- 1 tablespoon adobo sauce (from the can of chipotle peppers)
- 1 teaspoon dried oregano
- 1/2 teaspoon ground cumin
- Salt and pepper to taste
- Lime wedges, for serving
- Chopped cilantro, for garnish (optional)
- Cooked rice or warm tortillas, for serving

Instructions:

1. In a large skillet or saucepan, heat the vegetable oil over medium heat.
2. Add the finely chopped onion to the skillet and cook until softened and translucent, about 5 minutes.
3. Stir in the minced garlic and cook for another minute until fragrant.
4. Add the tomato puree or crushed tomatoes to the skillet, along with the chopped chipotle peppers, adobo sauce, dried oregano, ground cumin, salt, and pepper. Stir well to combine.
5. Bring the sauce to a simmer and let it cook for about 5-7 minutes, allowing the flavors to meld together and the sauce to thicken slightly.
6. Taste the sauce and adjust the seasoning or spiciness level if needed. Add more chipotle peppers or adobo sauce for extra heat, if desired.
7. Once the sauce is to your liking, add the peeled and deveined shrimp to the skillet, stirring to coat them evenly with the sauce.
8. Cook the shrimp in the sauce for 4-5 minutes, or until they are pink and opaque.
9. Remove the skillet from the heat and garnish the Camarones a la Diabla with chopped cilantro, if using.

10. Serve the spicy shrimp hot with lime wedges on the side for squeezing over the top. You can also serve them with cooked rice or warm tortillas to soak up the delicious sauce.

Enjoy the bold and spicy flavors of Camarones a la Diabla as a satisfying main dish for dinner! Adjust the level of spiciness according to your taste preferences.

Pozole Verde

Ingredients:

For the Pozole:

- 1 lb (about 450g) pork shoulder or pork butt, cut into small chunks
- 1 can (29 oz/822g) hominy, drained and rinsed
- 1 onion, chopped
- 4 cloves garlic, minced
- 6 cups (1.5 liters) chicken broth
- Salt and pepper to taste

For the Green Sauce:

- 1 lb (about 450g) fresh tomatillos, husks removed and rinsed
- 2-3 poblano peppers, seeded and roughly chopped
- 2 jalapeño peppers, seeded (optional, for extra heat)
- 1 bunch cilantro, stems removed
- 1 onion, chopped
- 4 cloves garlic, peeled
- 1 teaspoon ground cumin
- 1 teaspoon dried oregano
- Salt to taste
- Juice of 1 lime (optional, for added freshness)

For Serving:

- Sliced radishes
- Chopped cilantro
- Thinly sliced cabbage or lettuce
- Lime wedges
- Avocado slices
- Tortilla chips or tostadas

Instructions:

1. Start by preparing the pork. Season the pork chunks with salt and pepper.
2. In a large pot or Dutch oven, heat a bit of oil over medium-high heat. Brown the pork in batches until golden brown on all sides. Remove the pork from the pot and set aside.
3. In the same pot, add a bit more oil if needed. Add the chopped onion and minced garlic. Sauté until softened and fragrant, about 3-4 minutes.
4. Return the browned pork to the pot. Add the drained hominy and chicken broth. Bring the mixture to a boil, then reduce the heat to low. Cover and simmer for about 1 to 1.5 hours, or until the pork is tender and fully cooked.
5. While the pork is simmering, prepare the green sauce. In a blender or food processor, combine the tomatillos, poblano peppers, jalapeño peppers (if using), cilantro, chopped onion, garlic, ground cumin, dried oregano, and salt. Blend until smooth.
6. Once the pork is tender, stir in the green sauce. Simmer for an additional 15-20 minutes to allow the flavors to meld together.
7. Taste and adjust the seasoning with salt and lime juice, if desired, for added freshness.
8. Serve the Pozole Verde hot, garnished with sliced radishes, chopped cilantro, thinly sliced cabbage or lettuce, lime wedges, avocado slices, and tortilla chips or tostadas on the side for dipping or crumbling over the stew.

Enjoy the hearty and flavorful Pozole Verde as a comforting meal, perfect for chilly days or festive gatherings!

Huevos Rancheros

Ingredients:

- 4 large eggs
- 4 corn or flour tortillas
- 1 cup (240ml) canned or homemade refried beans
- 1 cup (240ml) salsa or homemade tomato-chili sauce
- 1/2 cup (60g) shredded cheese (such as cheddar or Monterey Jack)
- 1 avocado, sliced (optional)
- Chopped fresh cilantro, for garnish (optional)
- Lime wedges, for serving (optional)

Instructions:

1. Heat the tortillas: Warm the tortillas in a dry skillet over medium heat, flipping them occasionally until they are soft and pliable. Alternatively, you can heat them in the microwave wrapped in a damp paper towel for about 30 seconds.
2. Prepare the eggs: In a separate skillet, fry or scramble the eggs according to your preference. Season with salt and pepper to taste.
3. Warm the refried beans: Heat the refried beans in a small saucepan over low heat until warmed through. Stir occasionally to prevent sticking.
4. Assemble the Huevos Rancheros: Place a warm tortilla on each serving plate. Spread a layer of warmed refried beans on top of each tortilla.
5. Top the beans with the cooked eggs.
6. Spoon salsa or tomato-chili sauce over the eggs.
7. Sprinkle shredded cheese over the salsa.
8. If desired, garnish with sliced avocado and chopped fresh cilantro.
9. Serve the Huevos Rancheros hot, with lime wedges on the side for squeezing over the top.
10. Enjoy your delicious homemade Huevos Rancheros for breakfast or brunch!

Feel free to customize this recipe by adding additional toppings such as sliced jalapeños, diced onions, or sour cream. Serve with warm cornbread or potatoes for a hearty and satisfying meal.

Pan de Muerto

Ingredients:

For the bread:

- 4 cups (500g) all-purpose flour
- 1/2 cup (100g) granulated sugar
- 1/2 teaspoon salt
- 2 1/4 teaspoons active dry yeast (1 packet)
- 1/2 cup (120ml) milk
- 1/2 cup (120ml) water
- 1/2 cup (115g) unsalted butter, cubed
- 4 large eggs, beaten
- 1 teaspoon orange zest
- 1/4 cup (60ml) orange juice
- 1/4 cup (60ml) orange liqueur (such as Cointreau or Grand Marnier) - optional
- Additional flour for dusting

For the topping:

- 1/4 cup (50g) granulated sugar
- 1/4 cup (60ml) orange juice
- 1/4 cup (60g) unsalted butter, melted
- Additional granulated sugar for sprinkling

Instructions:

1. In a large mixing bowl, combine 2 cups of flour, sugar, salt, and yeast. Mix well.
2. In a small saucepan, heat the milk, water, and cubed butter over low heat until the butter is melted and the mixture is warm (about 110°F/45°C).
3. Gradually add the warm milk mixture to the dry ingredients, mixing until well combined.
4. Add the beaten eggs, orange zest, orange juice, and orange liqueur (if using). Stir until a sticky dough forms.

5. Gradually add the remaining 2 cups of flour, kneading the dough until it becomes smooth and elastic, about 8-10 minutes. You can do this by hand on a floured surface or with a stand mixer fitted with a dough hook attachment.
6. Place the dough in a greased bowl, cover it with a clean kitchen towel or plastic wrap, and let it rise in a warm place until doubled in size, about 1-2 hours.
7. Once the dough has risen, punch it down and divide it into portions, shaping them into round balls. You can make one large round loaf or smaller individual loaves.
8. Place the shaped dough balls onto a baking sheet lined with parchment paper. Cover them loosely with a clean kitchen towel and let them rise again for another 30-60 minutes.
9. Preheat your oven to 350°F (175°C).
10. In a small saucepan, heat the orange juice and sugar for the topping over low heat until the sugar is dissolved.
11. Once the dough balls have risen again, gently brush them with melted butter, then brush them with the orange juice and sugar mixture.
12. Bake the Pan de Muerto in the preheated oven for 20-25 minutes, or until golden brown and cooked through.
13. Remove the bread from the oven and let it cool slightly on a wire rack.
14. Optional: Sprinkle the warm Pan de Muerto with additional granulated sugar while still slightly warm.
15. Serve the Pan de Muerto warm or at room temperature, and enjoy this delicious and symbolic bread as part of your Día de los Muertos celebration!

Feel free to customize this recipe by adding additional flavors such as cinnamon or anise seeds to the dough. The orange zest and juice can also be substituted with lemon for a slightly different flavor profile.

Frijoles Charros

Ingredients:

- 1 lb (about 450g) dried pinto beans, sorted and rinsed
- 6 cups (1.5 liters) water
- 8 oz (about 225g) bacon, chopped
- 1 onion, finely chopped
- 2 cloves garlic, minced
- 1 jalapeño pepper, seeded and chopped (adjust to taste)
- 1 can (14.5 oz/411g) diced tomatoes, drained
- 2 cups (480ml) chicken or vegetable broth
- 1 teaspoon ground cumin
- 1 teaspoon dried oregano
- Salt and pepper to taste
- Chopped fresh cilantro, for garnish (optional)
- Lime wedges, for serving (optional)

Instructions:

1. In a large pot or Dutch oven, combine the dried pinto beans and water. Bring to a boil over high heat.
2. Reduce the heat to low, cover the pot, and let the beans simmer for about 1 to 1.5 hours, or until they are tender. Stir occasionally and add more water if needed to keep the beans submerged.
3. In a separate skillet, cook the chopped bacon over medium heat until it starts to render its fat and becomes slightly crispy.
4. Add the finely chopped onion to the skillet with the bacon and cook until the onion is softened and translucent, about 5 minutes.
5. Stir in the minced garlic and chopped jalapeño pepper, and cook for another minute until fragrant.
6. Add the drained diced tomatoes to the skillet and cook for a few minutes to soften them.
7. Once the beans are tender, add the cooked bacon mixture to the pot with the beans, along with the chicken or vegetable broth, ground cumin, and dried oregano. Stir well to combine.

8. Season the Frijoles Charros with salt and pepper to taste. Simmer the beans for an additional 15-20 minutes to allow the flavors to meld together.
9. Taste and adjust the seasoning if needed.
10. Serve the Frijoles Charros hot, garnished with chopped fresh cilantro and accompanied by lime wedges for squeezing over the top, if desired.

Enjoy the rich and savory flavors of Frijoles Charros as a satisfying and comforting dish, perfect for sharing with friends and family!

Mexican Fruit Salad (Ensalada de Frutas)

Ingredients:

- 2 cups (about 300g) cubed watermelon
- 1 cup (about 150g) diced pineapple
- 1 cup (about 150g) sliced strawberries
- 1 cup (about 150g) diced mango
- 1 cup (about 150g) diced jicama
- 1 cucumber, peeled and diced
- 2 tablespoons freshly squeezed lime juice
- 1 teaspoon chili powder (such as Tajín)
- Pinch of salt
- Fresh mint leaves for garnish (optional)

Instructions:

1. In a large mixing bowl, combine the cubed watermelon, diced pineapple, sliced strawberries, diced mango, diced jicama, and diced cucumber.
2. Drizzle the freshly squeezed lime juice over the fruit.
3. Sprinkle the chili powder and a pinch of salt over the fruit.
4. Gently toss the fruit salad until all the ingredients are well combined and evenly coated with the lime juice, chili powder, and salt.
5. Taste the fruit salad and adjust the seasoning if needed, adding more lime juice, chili powder, or salt according to your taste preferences.
6. Transfer the Mexican Fruit Salad to a serving bowl or individual serving dishes.
7. If desired, garnish the fruit salad with fresh mint leaves for a pop of color and added freshness.
8. Serve the Mexican Fruit Salad immediately, or cover and refrigerate it for up to a few hours to allow the flavors to meld together before serving.

Enjoy this vibrant and flavorful Mexican Fruit Salad as a refreshing and healthy snack, side dish, or dessert on a hot day or as part of a festive meal! It's perfect for summer gatherings, picnics, or anytime you're craving a light and refreshing treat.

Quesadillas

Ingredients:

- 4 large flour tortillas
- 2 cups (about 200g) shredded cheese (such as cheddar, Monterey Jack, or a blend)
- Optional fillings:
    - Cooked chicken, beef, or pork, shredded
    - Sauteed vegetables (such as bell peppers, onions, and mushrooms)
    - Refried beans
    - Cooked beans (such as black beans or pinto beans)
    - Sliced jalapeños or green chilies
    - Diced tomatoes or salsa
    - Cooked spinach or kale
    - Avocado slices
    - Cooked bacon or chorizo
    - Cilantro, chopped
    - Sour cream, guacamole, or salsa for serving

Instructions:

1. Preheat a large skillet or griddle over medium heat.
2. Place a tortilla on a flat surface. Sprinkle about 1/2 cup of shredded cheese evenly over one half of the tortilla.
3. If using any additional fillings, layer them on top of the cheese.
4. Fold the tortilla in half to cover the filling, creating a half-moon shape.
5. Carefully transfer the filled tortilla to the preheated skillet or griddle.
6. Cook the quesadilla for 2-3 minutes on each side, or until the tortilla is golden brown and crispy, and the cheese is melted.
7. Remove the cooked quesadilla from the skillet and place it on a cutting board.
8. Repeat the process with the remaining tortillas and filling ingredients.
9. Once all the quesadillas are cooked, use a sharp knife or pizza cutter to slice each quesadilla into wedges.
10. Serve the quesadillas hot, accompanied by sour cream, guacamole, salsa, or your favorite dipping sauces.

Enjoy your delicious homemade quesadillas as a snack, appetizer, or main dish! Feel free to get creative with the fillings and customize them to your taste preferences.

Chicharrón en Salsa Verde

Ingredients:

- 1 lb (about 450g) chicharrón (crispy pork skin), cut into bite-sized pieces
- 1 lb (about 450g) tomatillos, husked and rinsed
- 2-3 serrano or jalapeño peppers, stemmed (adjust to taste)
- 1 onion, peeled and chopped
- 2 cloves garlic, peeled
- 1/2 cup (120ml) chicken broth or water
- 1/2 cup (120ml) chopped fresh cilantro
- Salt to taste
- 2 tablespoons vegetable oil

Instructions:

1. In a large skillet or saucepan, heat the vegetable oil over medium heat.
2. Add the chopped onion and whole serrano or jalapeño peppers to the skillet. Cook until the vegetables are softened and slightly charred, about 5-7 minutes.
3. Meanwhile, in a separate pot, bring water to a boil. Add the tomatillos to the boiling water and cook for about 5 minutes, until they turn a darker shade of green and soften slightly.
4. Drain the tomatillos and transfer them to a blender or food processor. Add the cooked onion and peppers, along with the garlic cloves, chopped cilantro, and chicken broth or water.
5. Blend the ingredients until smooth, then season the salsa verde with salt to taste.
6. In the same skillet used to cook the onion and peppers, add the chicharrón pieces.
7. Pour the salsa verde over the chicharrón, stirring to coat the pieces evenly.
8. Bring the mixture to a simmer over medium heat, then reduce the heat to low. Let it simmer gently for about 10-15 minutes, stirring occasionally, to allow the flavors to meld together and the chicharrón to absorb the salsa.
9. Taste and adjust the seasoning with salt if needed.
10. Once the Chicharrón en Salsa Verde is heated through and the flavors have developed, remove the skillet from the heat.
11. Serve the Chicharrón en Salsa Verde hot, accompanied by warm tortillas, rice, or beans.

Enjoy this savory and comforting Mexican dish as a satisfying main course or as part of a larger meal!

Aguachile

Ingredients:

- 1 lb (about 450g) large shrimp, peeled and deveined
- 1 cup (240ml) freshly squeezed lime juice
- 2-3 serrano or jalapeño peppers, stemmed and thinly sliced (adjust to taste)
- 1/2 red onion, thinly sliced
- 1 cucumber, thinly sliced
- 1/4 cup (60ml) chopped cilantro
- Salt to taste
- Optional garnishes: sliced avocado, sliced radishes, extra cilantro leaves, lime wedges, tostadas or tortilla chips

Instructions:

1. Start by preparing the shrimp. If using frozen shrimp, thaw them completely and drain any excess moisture. Peel and devein the shrimp, then rinse them under cold water and pat them dry with paper towels.
2. In a large mixing bowl, combine the peeled and deveined shrimp with the freshly squeezed lime juice. Make sure the shrimp are fully submerged in the lime juice. Let them marinate in the lime juice for about 15-20 minutes. The acidity of the lime juice will "cook" the shrimp slightly.
3. While the shrimp are marinating, prepare the other ingredients. Thinly slice the serrano or jalapeño peppers, red onion, and cucumber. Chop the cilantro.
4. After the shrimp have marinated, add the sliced serrano or jalapeño peppers, red onion, cucumber, and chopped cilantro to the bowl with the shrimp and lime juice.
5. Season the Aguachile with salt to taste, and toss everything together gently to combine.
6. Let the Aguachile marinate in the refrigerator for an additional 10-15 minutes to allow the flavors to meld together.
7. Once ready to serve, divide the Aguachile among serving plates or bowls. Optionally, garnish with sliced avocado, sliced radishes, extra cilantro leaves, and lime wedges.
8. Serve the Aguachile immediately, accompanied by tostadas or tortilla chips for scooping up the flavorful mixture.

Enjoy the spicy, tangy, and refreshing flavors of Aguachile as a delightful appetizer or light meal, perfect for warm weather or any occasion! Adjust the level of spiciness according to your taste preferences.

Capirotada (Mexican Bread Pudding)

Ingredients:

- 6 cups (about 400g) stale bolillo or French bread, cut into cubes
- 1 cup (about 100g) shredded Monterey Jack or Chihuahua cheese
- 1 cup (about 150g) raisins
- 1 cup (about 150g) chopped walnuts or pecans
- 1 cup (about 150g) dried apricots, chopped
- 1 cup (about 150g) dried figs, chopped
- 1 cup (about 150g) piloncillo or dark brown sugar
- 2 cinnamon sticks
- 4 cloves
- 4 cups (960ml) water
- 1/4 cup (60ml) unsalted butter
- Optional garnishes: vanilla ice cream, whipped cream, or additional nuts and dried fruit for topping

Instructions:

1. Preheat your oven to 350°F (175°C).
2. In a large saucepan, combine the piloncillo or dark brown sugar, cinnamon sticks, cloves, and water. Bring the mixture to a boil over medium heat, stirring occasionally, until the piloncillo or sugar is dissolved. Reduce the heat and let the syrup simmer for about 10-15 minutes to infuse the flavors.
3. While the syrup is simmering, assemble the Capirotada. In a large baking dish, layer half of the bread cubes, followed by half of the shredded cheese, raisins, chopped nuts, dried apricots, and dried figs. Repeat the layers with the remaining ingredients, ending with a layer of cheese on top.
4. Once the syrup is ready, remove the cinnamon sticks and cloves. Stir in the unsalted butter until melted.
5. Pour the hot syrup evenly over the assembled Capirotada in the baking dish, making sure to moisten all the bread cubes.
6. Cover the baking dish with aluminum foil and bake in the preheated oven for about 30-40 minutes, or until the bread pudding is hot and bubbly, and the cheese is melted and slightly golden on top.

7. Remove the foil and continue to bake for an additional 10-15 minutes, or until the top is golden brown and crispy.
8. Once done, remove the Capirotada from the oven and let it cool slightly before serving.
9. Serve the Capirotada warm, optionally topped with vanilla ice cream, whipped cream, or additional nuts and dried fruit for extra flavor and texture.

Enjoy the rich and comforting flavors of this classic Mexican dessert, perfect for special occasions or anytime you're craving a sweet and satisfying treat!

Chicken Tinga

Ingredients:

- 1 lb (about 450g) boneless, skinless chicken breasts or thighs
- 2 tablespoons vegetable oil
- 1 onion, finely chopped
- 2 cloves garlic, minced
- 1 can (14 oz/400g) diced tomatoes
- 2-3 chipotle peppers in adobo sauce, chopped (adjust to taste)
- 2 tablespoons adobo sauce (from the can of chipotle peppers)
- 1 teaspoon dried oregano
- 1/2 teaspoon ground cumin
- Salt and pepper to taste
- Corn tortillas, for serving
- Optional toppings: diced avocado, shredded lettuce, chopped cilantro, crumbled queso fresco, lime wedges

Instructions:

1. In a large skillet or saucepan, heat the vegetable oil over medium heat.
2. Add the finely chopped onion to the skillet and cook until softened and translucent, about 5 minutes.
3. Stir in the minced garlic and cook for another minute until fragrant.
4. Add the diced tomatoes (with their juices) to the skillet, along with the chopped chipotle peppers, adobo sauce, dried oregano, and ground cumin. Stir well to combine.
5. Season the sauce with salt and pepper to taste.
6. Add the boneless, skinless chicken breasts or thighs to the skillet, making sure they are submerged in the sauce.
7. Cover the skillet and let the chicken simmer in the sauce for about 20-25 minutes, or until the chicken is cooked through and tender.
8. Once the chicken is cooked, remove it from the skillet and shred it using two forks.
9. Return the shredded chicken to the skillet and stir it into the sauce until well coated.

10. Let the Chicken Tinga simmer for an additional 5-10 minutes to allow the flavors to meld together.
11. Taste and adjust the seasoning if needed.
12. Serve the Chicken Tinga warm, spooned onto warm corn tortillas.
13. Optionally, garnish the Chicken Tinga with diced avocado, shredded lettuce, chopped cilantro, crumbled queso fresco, and lime wedges for squeezing over the top.

Enjoy the smoky, tangy, and spicy flavors of Chicken Tinga as a delicious filling for tacos, tostadas, or tortas! It's a versatile dish that's sure to be a hit with family and friends.